# Mother Pletsch's
# PAINLESS SEWING

with Pretty Pati's Perfect Pattern Prir...

IV

D0499500

## and Ample Annie's Awful, but Adequate Artwork!

### by Pati Palmer and Susan Pletsch

We'd like to dedicate this book to all of our crazy friends including eleven year old Julie who for the sake of alliteration gave us our crazy nicknames and.....hence a title for our book.

CARTOONIST

JO REID

Technical artwork by the authors.

Copyright © 1975 by Pati Palmer and Susan Pletsch.
Second printing and update, 1977. Third printing and update 1979. Fourth printing 1980. Fifth printing 1981.
Published by Palmer/Pletsch Associates
Printed by GlassDahlstrom GraphicPress, Portland, Oregon U.S.A.

Whenever brand names are mentioned, it is only to indicate to the consumer products we have personally tested and have been pleased with. We are not subsidized by anyone. There may very well be other products that are comparable or even better to aid you in your sewing or that may be developed after the printing of this book.

ISBN 0-935278-00-1

About the authors . . . . . .

Pati Palmer and Susan Pletsch, two talented home economists, have developed careers promoting a favorite hobby, home sewing. They have co-authored four sewing books, have established their own publishing company, and now travel across the U.S. teaching seminars based on the Palmer/Pletsch books. They also consult with the fabric and notions companies. Their most recent accomplishments include designing patterns for Vogue and McCall's and creating and starring in an educational film based on a Palmer/Pletsch book.

Pati Palmer

Pati and Susan met as educational representatives for Armo Co., a shaping manufacturer. Pati has also been Corporate Home Economist for an Oregon department store, as well as buyer of sewing notions. Pati graduated from Ore. State University with a B.S. in Home Economics. She is active in the American Home Economics Association, Home Economists in Business, and Fashion Group.

Susan Pletsch

Susan has been a home economist with Talon Consumer Education, where she traveled extensively giving workshops. She was also a free-lance home economist with many sewing related firms. Susan graduated from Arizona State University in home economics and taught home economics to special education students. She is active in the American Home Economics Association and Home Economists in Business.

Pati and Susan are individually recognized for their sewing skills and teaching and lecturing abilities. Together they produce an unbeatable combination of knowledge, personality and talent.

.......and their friends......

Ample Annie is Ann Peterson who left an "8 to 5" job to begin her own custom uniform factory (located in her second bedroom!). Her first contract was for 150 band uniforms, which she designed and sewed herself in less than four weeks. Imagine this---making 1200 buttonholes---sewing on 1200 buttons---AND---setting in 300 sleeves. Annie is our resident expert in daredevil speed.

Speedy but elegant describes the sewing methods used by Marta McCoy Alto, past costume mistress and super-custom seamstress who now teaches very special sewing classes in Portland. Marta sews faster and yet better than anyone else we know. She has the magic touch in turning fabric into a couture garment overnight.

Ample Annie's sister Jo Reid is actually our inspired cartoonist. Annie had the idea---but Jo has the touch. Jo, an art education graduate from Oregon College of Education, was once a sewing "dropout," but has since reconsidered and is giving it another chance.

# TABLE OF CONTENTS

# But I don't have the patience to sew...

    <u>Mother Pletsch's Painless Sewing</u> will not try to convince you that you should sew---that's your own decision. But for all of the rest of us who are hooked on sewing, there is hope. <u>There is an easier way</u>!

    We learned to sew in the same ways as many of you---from our mothers and home economics teachers ---and our teachers were possibly no better or worse than yours. So why are we loving our hobby and profession of sewing while you curse the same?

Forty years of combined experience helps. (We started to sew as very small children!!) But the real answers are attitudes, believing in the power of positive thinking, and insisting on finding the easier way. We are incurable optimists. We always will look at a half glass of wine and say it is half full. The power of positive thinking lives in sewing too. If you think the dress is going to be gorgeous---it will be! Or we will help you find a way to make it gorgeous.

We feel that sewing is such a personal and an individual thing that there simply cannot be a "right" way to complete a given task. We find that even we often disagree on the easiest or best way because we are two different people. So, whenever necessary, we will illustrate more than one way. Be flexible and try them all. Remember that finding a method that's easy for you is somewhat like buying new shoes. Unless you try on every possible pair, you will never know if you bought the most comfortable ones.

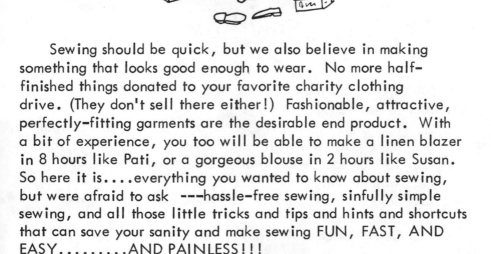

Sewing should be quick, but we also believe in making something that looks good enough to wear. No more half-finished things donated to your favorite charity clothing drive. (They don't sell there either!) Fashionable, attractive, perfectly-fitting garments are the desirable end product. With a bit of experience, you too will be able to make a linen blazer in 8 hours like Pati, or a gorgeous blouse in 2 hours like Susan. So here it is....everything you wanted to know about sewing, but were afraid to ask ---hassle-free sewing, sinfully simple sewing, and all those little tricks and tips and hints and shortcuts that can save your sanity and make sewing FUN, FAST, AND EASY.........AND PAINLESS!!!

# How to Sew Fast!

Speedy sewing is an art.  Like singing ability, some people naturally have it and some don't.  But also like singing, it is possible for us to discipline ourselves to do better. Study "How to Sew Fast" and force yourself to follow our suggestions for ONE MONTH and see if you can't improve your sewing speed.

READY, SET, .... SEW!!!!!

THE DAREDEVIL SEAMSTRESS SPEAKS:  Ample Annie says, "In order to sew fast....."

1. Turn off all music, TV, and radio noise while cutting out a pattern---that is when you need to concentrate.
2. Turn on speedy banjo or intense Beethoven music when sewing.
3. Take the telephone off the hook until you are ready to do handwork.
4. Drink coffee with sugar or eat cookies for energy.

# HOW TO SEW FAST:   TEN TIPS

1. <u>Cut your fabric with right sides together</u> so all **center front and center back seams** are in a ready-to-sew position.

2. <u>Snips - not notches.</u> When cutting, keep marking and pinning to a minimum by using a 1/4" snip into the seam allowance to indicate a notch. We have often been told not to clip into a seam allowance because we may need to let out the seam, but if you need to get into that last 1/4", you are in deep trouble anyway. So...<u>snip-mark</u> center front, center back, notches, top of sleeves, and other "joining" points.

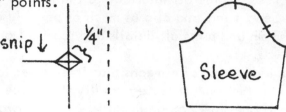

3. <u>Put your foot on the accelerator</u> and FORCE your machine to sew fast.  It does take somewhat slower stitching to do smooth curves, but learn to sew as fast as your machine will stitch on all straight seams, in staystitching, and in zig-zag seam finishing. Sewing fast will not hurt your machine---in fact, it is actually better for it. Constant slow sewing is like driving your car and never shifting out of first gear!

4. <u>Continuous sewing.</u> It takes time and thread to stop at the end of each seam, clip threads and start over. Instead, stitch immediately from one seam to another. Use continuous sewing when:
   1. Staystitching
   2. Sewing seams *
   3. Zig-zag seam finishing

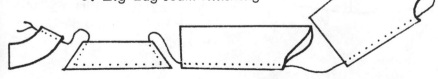

*You may still backstitch where you normally would when continuous stitching.

5. Consolidated sewing - "Press as you sew" is a super idea, but we would all have wrestler's thighs from getting up each time we needed to press one seam. Save time and your thigh muscles by sewing as many seams as possible before going to the iron. Stop sewing only when you have to cross another seam that should be pressed open first. Do as much as possible at one time.

- Cut everything at one time including interfacings and linings.
- Mark everything you can at the cutting table.
- Fuse or glue all interfacings in place at one time.
- Sew, trim, and clip as much as possible at one time.
- Turn and press all details and seams at one time.

Consolidated sewing also means that it is easier to make two shirts at the same time, especially if you use the same pattern. If one shirt can be made in 2 hours, two shirts can be made in 3 hours.

6. Flat First! This means to complete flat pieces before joining side seams. It's not easy to sew in a tube. For example, put the zipper in the back pieces and sew the darts before sewing the side seams.

Put pockets on shirt fronts before joining to back

Sew collar to a dress neckline before sewing the side seams.

7. <u>Jam-proof sewing</u> means holding onto the upper thread for the first 3 – 4 stitches in a seam. This is a preventative measure. It prevents jammed threads which take time to unjam and also saves frustration. (Jamming is most common in zig-zag machines with the larger hole in the throat plate.)

8. <u>Taut sewing</u>---a super new technique that allows any number of layers and weights of fabrics to feed evenly through the machine with no machine adjustments. Pull equally on your fabric in front of and behind the needle as you sew. Do not stretch, just pull until "taut" as if you were sewing with your fabric in an embroidery hoop. However, let the fabric feed through the machine on its own.

> <u>NOTE:</u> Taut sewing is automatic pucker prevention. Use it when sewing Qiana, Ultrasuede, permanent press fabrics, and velvet.

9. <u>Tie threads?? No No!!</u> Try one of the following methods instead:
   - ....Knot in place by lifting the presser foot 1/8" and holding onto the fabric with a finger on each side of the presser foot so the fabric won't move, and stitch in place 3 or 4 times.

   - ....Turn your machine to "0" stitch length, stitch 3 or 4 times in place.

   - ....Drop feed dogs to stitch 3 or 4 times in place.

   - ....Of course you can always backstitch 3 or 4 stitches over your original stitching line.

10. <u>The obvious ---know your machine.</u> Learn to use it to the fullest. If you don't know how to use the buttonholer, for example, sit down at the machine for 30 minutes making non-stop buttonholes in a scrap of fabric. We guarantee that you'll learn to make excellent machine buttonholes if you do this.

Now that we have given you a few tips on how to sew faster, we are going to skip all those other "cutesy" little ideas for the moment and talk about a "concept" of sewing that is much more important than any single tip---ORGANIZATION!

1. ORGANIZATION in sewing habits (see tips 1 through 10)
2. ORGANIZATION of your sewing room and tools.
3. ORGANIZATION of shopping and wardrobe planning.

## ROOM AND TOOLS

Ideally, a sewing room, closet, or corner should have the following:
1. Mug rack on the wall.
2. Full length mirror.
3. Chest of drawers next to the machine for small supplies and storing fabric and notions -- and for your own personal interfacing "store."
4. Surface that can be used for both cutting and pressing and and that can remain set up at all times.
5. Waste basket or paper bag attached to machine.
6. Bulletin board (nice if above the machine to hold guide sheets).

Being able to close a door or put up a screen to hide the sewing area and to leave sewing out as projects are in progress is more than a luxury -- it is the way to sanity. The amount of space you have is not really an important factor, organization of that space is the real key. We know a woman who has a huge basement for a sewing room. It's like sewing in a football field. It takes her forever to complete one garment because things are so far apart. She has TOO MUCH ROOM.

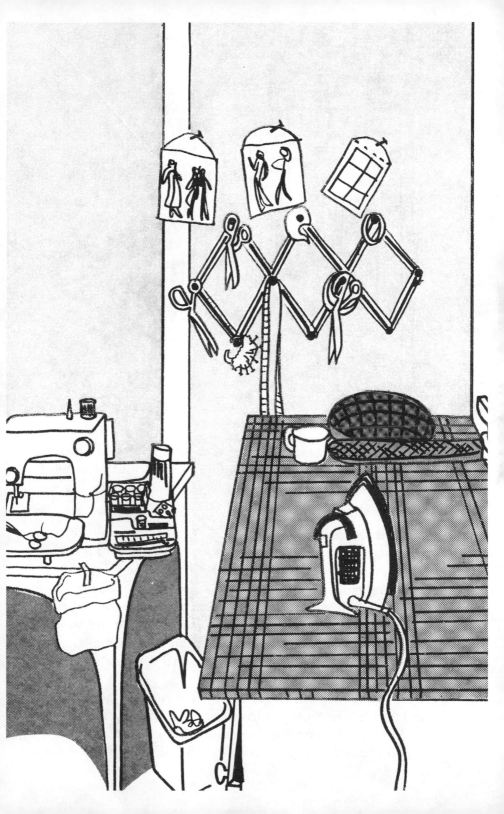

Do you have a closet full of clothes and nothing to wear? What a tragic waste of all the time spent sewing that closet-full. Wouldn't it be better to have spent 1/2 the time making 1/2 the clothes and yet still have TWICE as much to wear?

## Coordinate and Consolidate

...Don't be a pack rat. Get rid of what you don't wear, then you won't feel guilty about making new things.

...Planning makes the most of the sewing time you do have. When you coordinate, one blouse can go with 4 outfits, and you don't have to make 4 different blouses.

...Pick one or two base colors and plan around these. They don't have to be basic blue or brown. Choose magenta or tangerine if that thrills you!

...Don't be a remnant queen. Buy 8 yards of a good solid-colored fabric that you love and make pants, skirt, jacket, and vest. Then accessorize and mix and match. It saves $$$ and saves shopping time and SAVES SEWING TIME.

...Carry color swatches with you! Buy one of those little plastic accordian fold wallet photo holders for swatches and favorite pattern yardage requirements. Look at it every time you make a fabric or accessory purchase and slap your hands if it doesn't fit into the "grand scheme of things."

## SMART SHOPPING SAVES TIME, MONEY, AND HASSLE

1. Solid colors are more versatile and faster to sew than plaids. Also, prints that don't require matching are fast to sew because they hide all kinds of mistakes and make a simple pattern look smashing. FOR SPEED, AVOID PLAIDS -- they look great, but require cutting concentration. They are not in the fast category. Wool and wool/blend tweeds are probably the fastest to sew because they hide mistakes and press and mold to shape easily.

2. Buy the best quality fabric you can afford. It will be easier to sew and will reward you by looking like a million dollars for years. Besides, you're going to have fewer items to wear, so what you have must be more durable.

3. Buying patterns takes time -- make every pattern up at least twice to save looking time and sewing time PLUS $$$. Different fabrics change the whole look of a pattern anyway. Susan has made the same shirt 23 times! The same $3.50 pattern includes a beautifully classic blazer that both Pati and Susan have made up a combined grand total of 18 times. The pattern is 4 years old, still fashion-right, and has been backed with fusible interfacing to preserve the tissue paper for another 4 years.

4. If you're going to copy ready-to-wear, copy the best! Go to the custom or designer shops to snoop-shop. Try it on and see if it's you. Don't copy basement ideas. It's a waste of your precious time and talent.

5. Don't waste time making something you can afford to buy unless you can't get a good fit or the right color.

# From Fiber to Fabric

If you feel you already have a good understanding of the selection and care of all the fibers and fabrics that are on the market, don't bother reading this chapter -- that wouldn't be painless sewing. But if you are unsure...

FIBERS -- a fiber is a fine hair-like substance that is used in making yarns that are woven or knitted into fabrics.

> Generic names -- a name of a "family" of fibers similar in composition such as polyester or nylon.

> Brand names -- first names given to fibers by the chemical companies that make them. For example, DuPont named one of its polyester fibers "Dacron."

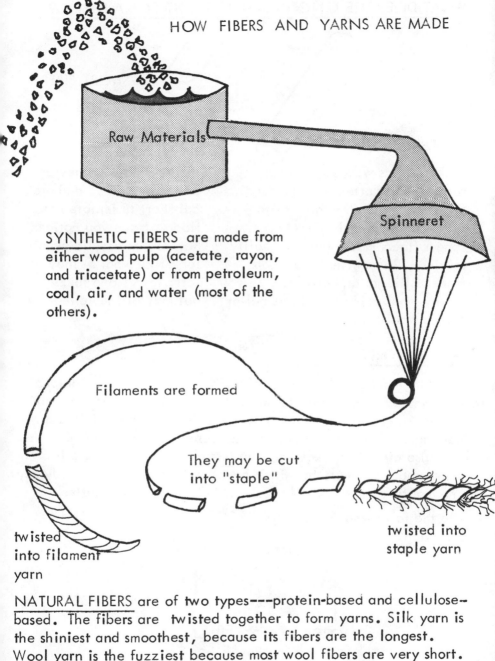

Raw Materials

Spinneret

SYNTHETIC FIBERS are made from either wood pulp (acetate, rayon, and triacetate) or from petroleum, coal, air, and water (most of the others).

Filaments are formed

They may be cut into "staple"

twisted into filament yarn

twisted into staple yarn

NATURAL FIBERS are of two types---protein-based and cellulose-based. The fibers are twisted together to form yarns. Silk yarn is the shiniest and smoothest, because its fibers are the longest. Wool yarn is the fuzziest because most wool fibers are very short. Protein fibers ---silk (unwound from the silkworm's cocoon) and wool (short fibers from the fleece of a sheep) Cellulose fibers--- linen (from the stems of the flax plant) and cotton (made from the seed pod of the cotton plant)

17

# WHAT DOES THE LENGTH OF A FIBER DO FOR A FABRIC?

LONG FIBERS · SHORT FIBERS

Make fabrics with smoother surfaces that often wear better. If SYNTHETIC, the fabrics are often stronger. If NATURAL, longer fibers make the best quality fabrics. They wrinkle less, are more resilient, and pill less. This is why wool gabardine wears better than a wool flannel.

If SYNTHETIC, they are called "staple," and are cut short to imitate natural fibers. Have you noticed how Orlon acrylic sweaters look like wool? They are soft, lofty, and fuzzy, but may pill more readily.

## FIBER ABSORBENCY

The moisture absorbency of a fiber is an important factor in wear and care. The more absorbent fibers are more comfortable to wear, because they pick up body moisture and humidity. Since they absorb moisture, they are less prone to static electricity and will also clean more easily. The less absorbent fibers are less comfortable to wear, but since they are less affected by body heat and moisture, they wrinkle less and hold their shape better.

Use the following ABSORBENCY SCALE as a guide in fabric selection.

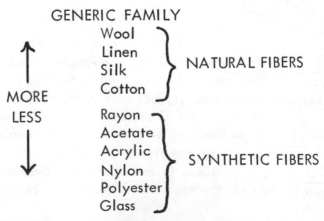

GENERIC FAMILY

| | |
|---|---|
| Wool | |
| Linen | NATURAL FIBERS |
| Silk | |
| Cotton | |

MORE
LESS

| | |
|---|---|
| Rayon | |
| Acetate | |
| Acrylic | |
| Nylon | SYNTHETIC FIBERS |
| Polyester | |
| Glass | |

18

Rayon, the most absorbent synthetic, is actually as absorbent as most of the natural fibers, but the other synthetics are all much less absorbent.

NOTE: Remember that this scale is true in 90% of the cases today, but if more altering is done to fibers such as in the use of the Visa finish, it will be less true.

## FIBER MODIFICATION

Why do some synthetics differ from others made from the same ingredients? "Fiber modification" means to change basic synthetic fibers by simply changing the shape of the hole that produces the fiber. Dacron VIII polyester has an octalobal cross-section because it is extruded from an 8 - sided hole.

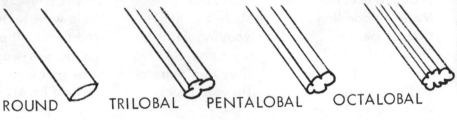

ROUND     TRILOBAL     PENTALOBAL     OCTALOBAL

Modification may change the characteristics of the fabric by making it.....

1. Less clingy and static prone
2. More resistant to soil
3. Breathe better (more channels for moisture)
4. Deeper, richer color
5. Less shine

## TEXTURIZING FOR STRETCH

Texturizing a synthetic filament yarn induces a coil or crimp that provides a stretch characteristic to a woven or knitted fabric. It also makes fabrics lighter weight and loftier.

This kind of texturizing can only be done to thermoplastic synthetic fibers such as nylon and polyester, because they have the ability to be softened and shaped or "heat set." It cannot be done to those made from wood pulp.

A TEXTURIZED YARN:

## FABRIC

The fibers and yarns we have been discussing can be made into a number of different fabrics.

  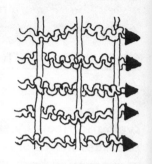

| NON-WOVENS | WOVENS | STRETCH-WOVENS |
|---|---|---|
| Made by bonding fibers together. They don't ravel. Some stretch, some don't and some stretch only in one direction. | Made by inter-weaving yarns at right angles. They don't stretch. They do ravel. | Made with textur-ized yarns. They may be one-way or two-way stretch. They do ravel. |

LOOPS VS. LINES --- whereas yarns in wovens run in straight lines across the fabric, knits are a series of interlocking loops. The main way to recognize knits is that they don't ravel.

SINGLE KNITS --- Made with a single needle. They stretch in both directions, have lengthwise "wales" on the right side and crosswise "courses" on the wrong sides, and roll to the right side when stretched on the cross grain. Sweater knits and tricots are popular varieties.

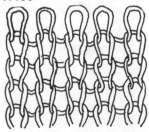

DOUBLEKNITS --- Made with more than one needle. Plain ones look the same on both sides. There are many varieties including the currently popular interlocks.

## SO WHAT IS THE BIG TEXTILE DEAL!

How does all this information help you? First decide what qualities are important for you to be happy with the finished product. For example, does a Halloween costume need to be high performance? Then, perform your own QQQ (Quick Quality Quiz) every time you buy a fabric.

### QQQ (Quick Quality Quiz)

1. <u>Will it wrinkle</u>?
   Perform the wrinkle test by holding a 5" square in your hand and squeeze it for five seconds. Do the wrinkles come out quickly? The higher a fiber is on the absorbency scale, the more it will wrinkle. Wovens generally wrinkle more than knits. Stretch wovens wrinkle less than regular wovens.

2. <u>Will it hold its shape</u>?
   The "thumb test" can be performed by pulling a small section of the fabric with your thumbs and holding for five seconds. If it recovers quickly from the warmth and stress of your thumbs, it will hold its shape in wear. The tighter the knit or weave, the heavier the fabric, and the less absorbent the fiber, the better it will hold its shape. Generally, double knits hold their shape better than single knits, wovens better than knits, and synthetics better than natural fibers.

3. <u>Will it pill</u>?
   The shorter the fibers, the more it is likely to pill. The less absorbent the fiber, the drier and more static-prone it will be and thus the short fibers will cling together, or "pill", more easily.

4. <u>Will it sew easily</u>?
   Knits don't ravel, so seam finishes are unnecessary. Very stretchy fabrics may be harder to handle as well as fabrics made from slippery filament fibers. Nonabsorbent fibers may not be able to be pressed flat easily.

5. <u>Will it be comfortable</u>?
   Fabrics that are lightweight and absorbent are often more comfortable to wear. Thick knits and nonabsorbent synthetics are often warm and feel clammy. HOWEVER, they wrinkle less.

21

# NOTABLE FABRICS AND NEW TERMS

VISA® -- a finish, patented by Milliken, that is applied to polyester fabrics to make them snag proof, more comfortable to wear, more absorbent, and easier to clean. Two fabrics that are especially nice with this finish are Milliken's 14 oz. polyester doubleknits and their stretch-woven polyesters. Both are excellent for pants. DuPont's Zelcon® is a similar finish.

INTERLOCK KNITS -- double knits that are lighter in weight and stretchier than most typical double knits, yet hang better than most jersey or tricot knits, because they are slightly thicker. They are mainly produced from polyester, nylon, or cotton yarns. Interlocks run lengthwise in one direction, but staystitching prevents runs. We usually put the direction that runs at the bottom and staystitch the hem edge. Tug on a cut edge to determine the direction of run. They should be cut in one direction like a napped fabric because of the way they reflect light. Use a ball point needle size 9/10 and polyester thread.

SILK -- No, it's not new, but you will be seeing more of it due to the returning demand for natural fibers, including luxurious silk.

Many silks are hand washable. However, satins, some crepe de chines and chiffons are best dry cleaned. Also, neon bright colors always last best when dry cleaned. We like to dry clean even washable silks every other time for longevity. Sew with a new size 9/10 (or 70) sewing machine needle and silk or cotton thread. Coats & Clark's extra fine polyester thread for lingerie also works well. Stitchable interfacings such as silk organza are recommended. We've used Easy Knit and Fuse-A-Knit fusibles on silk crepe de chine successfully, but always make a test sample first and wash it.

22

QIANA® NYLON -- It is appropriate to talk about this DuPont nylon with silk, as it is closer to silk than any other fiber. Qiana fiber is currently being made into single knits and double knits, velvets that are crush proof, and slinky wovens. It can be washed in hot water in the machine and looks good for years. Qiana breathes more than most nylons and will not turn grey or discolor in chlorinated water making it excellent for bathing suits.

STRETCH-WOVEN POLYESTERS -- woven fabrics with give. They can be found in both plain, twill, and satin weaves, and are usually 60" wide. They have the stretch and wrinkle resistance of knits but the look of wovens. Some new stretch-wovens even have the feel of wool because shorter fibers are mixed in with the long texturized filaments. An example is Steeplechase by Burlington/Klopman. Sew stretch-wovens with polyester thread.

NON-WOVENS -- Ultrasuede®, a 60% polyester and 40% polyurethane fabric, is one of the most famous non-wovens. It is durable, washable, and dry cleanable. It will not stretch, pill, crock, wrinkle, water spot, or stiffen like real suede. See Sewing Skinner® Ultrasuede® Fabric for sewing techniques. (Book ordering information on pg. 134.)

SPANDEX BLEND FABRICS -- Lycra is an example. Look for denim and corduroy blended with spandex for jeans that fit and feel great!

NATURAL BLEND™-- Cotton Incorporated's trademark for durable press fabrics of 60% or more cotton. It is a result of new technology that has shown that the amount of comfortable cotton can be increased in a garment without sacrificing performance.

FLAME RETARDANT FABRICS -- where a stiff ugly finish had been used in the past, now more permanent flame resistant fibers such as modacrylic, some polyesters, and some nylons are being utilized.

23

# TLC ... Textile Love and Care

## THE BASICS

1. Always read the bolt-end label for fiber type and care instructions. Request a permanent care label and sew it into the finished garment.
2. Always preshrink as you plan to care for the finished garment. Preshrink shaping fabrics (see pg. 41) and zippers at the same time.

She said pre-shrink EVERYTHING !!!

3. Since most fabrics today are synthetic or synthetic blends, follow these general instructions.

| HOW | WHY |
|---|---|
| 1. Use warm water | 1. Synthetics relax and lose wrinkles in warm water. Hot water may cause color loss in some. |

2. Don't overcrowd washing machine.

2. Crowding causes wrinkles and abrasion.

3. Use detergent when pre-shrinking fabric.

3. Softens fabric for maximum shrinkage.

4. Avoid cold water detergents if heavily chlorinated.

4. Hard on color.

5. Use cool rinse and short spin cycle.

5. Cools synthetics so wrinkles aren't set during spin cycle.

6. Remove from washer immediately.

6. Prevents wrinkling.

7. Use automatic dryer, but avoid overdrying.

7. Causes static electricity, progressive shrinkage, and loss of fabric life.

8. Good to use wash and wear or permanent press dryer setting.

8. Has cool down cycle to prevent wrinkling when dryer stops.

9. Remove from dryer immediately.

9. Prevents wrinkling.

10. Fabric softener in washer or dryer may be used.

10. Helps control static electricity as well as soften fabric.

NOTE: Save time in caring for the finished garment by leaving clothes on hangers until washed or dry cleaned.

## EXCEPTIONS

1. Fabrics that may lose their color.

Red and navy. Even though they don't "fade," they may seem to due to an overspray of dye. Test in sink before putting in with other clothes. Use cool water. White vinegar sometimes helps set dye.

Acetates. Many are dyed with less color fast dyes. Hand wash in lots of cool water. DON'T SOAK. Line or hangar dry.

Printed nylon tricot and jersey. Color doesn't always penetrate nonabsorbent fibers. Hand wash in cool water for longest life. Qiana is an exception.

2. 100% cotton knits.

Pre-shrink 3 times in washer and dryer. Shrinkage may occur each time. Some shrink as much as 5" per yard.

3. Wool.

> Hand wash in Woolite and cool water. Don't soak.
> Towel dry.
> Preshrink wool. We prefer to have it steamed by
> the dry cleaner if it is going to be dry-cleaned and pressed.
> We generally have our clothes cleaned only and don't
> bother to preshrink. So far...no trouble. Use woolens
> that are of good quality and "ready-for-the-needle."

4. Washable wool.

> Read the manufacturer's instructions.
> Machine wash on "wool" cycle in cool water.

5. Sewing notions.

> Zippers, seam tape, and trims are best preshrunk in
> the bathroom basin and line dried or placed in a mesh
> laundry bag or old nylon stocking to protect them in the
> washer and dryer.

6. Flame retardant fabrics.

> Launder them in a manner that will not render the finish
> inactive.
> DO NOT use soap or a fabric softener. They leave a
> fat residue that builds up on the fabric making the
> fabrics less flame retardant.
> DO NOT use chlorine bleach on cotton fabrics with a
> flame retardant finish.
> Use phosphate detergents or a non-phosphate heavy duty
> liquid detergent if phosphates are banned in your area.
> Warm water and low heat dryer cycles are best .

## STAIN REMOVAL -- TWO SUGGESTIONS

NOTE: Polyesters and many other synthetics have a bad habit---
they tend to absorb oil -borne stains. To salvage synthetics you
now have in your wardrobe, try spray laundry soil lifters
or make a detergent paste and pretreat the stain before laundering.
Washer and dryer heat can set a stain into the fiber if not carefully
pretreated.

NOTE: Ball point pen ink is another gremlin. Saturate the
stain with water soluble hair spray and blot with a paper
towel. Repeat until ink stain is gone. You will then have a
hair spray stain, but that washes out easily!

# Tools of the Trade

A craftsman is only as fine as his tools---an old but appropriate saying. Imagine what a lousy cook Julia Child might be if she had to cook dinner on a hot plate in a closet.

Would Julia Child cook dinner on a hot plate in a closet??

We really believe in investing in good quality basic tools and then in splurging occasionally on some sanity saving gadgets. Treat yourself---invest a little in your sewing now so you can sew painlessly for years to come!

27

## THE BASICS

1. <u>Tape measure</u> ---reinforced fiberglass won't stretch. The centimeter/inch tape measure would be helpful today, but essential tomorrow.

2. <u>Sewing gauge</u>--- a 6" ruler with a sliding marker. Super for marking hems and spacing buttons. Susan has two---one at the machine and one at the ironing board.

3. <u>Tracing wheel</u>---for marking darts quickly. The smooth edge wheel is the best variety for modern fabrics. It won't cut the fibers OR your pattern.

4. <u>Tracing paper</u>---try new washable Trace-B-Gone™ by Dritz.

5. <u>Tailors chalk with holder</u>---handier than a pencil because the holder has a built-in sharpening device and eraser brush.

6. <u>Thimble</u>---Susan feels this is optional and uses one only for sewing very heavy fabrics. Pati can't hand sew without one.

7. <u>Pins</u>---long, slender glass head pins (easy to locate when spilled) are the most basic and easiest on the hands when used. Good ones are hard to find. Try different brands until you come up with a good one. We found one that is labeled "ball point" that is nice for all fabrics.

8. <u>Magnet</u>---to retrieve pins spilled on your shag carpet.

9. <u>Singer Yellow Band</u>™ (#2045) sewing machine needles---seem to stop skipped stitches when all other attempts fail---even on Ultrasuede® and Qiana®.

10. <u>Cutting board</u>---the folding cardboard variety has 1" ruled lines on it for ease in "squaring" your fabric before cutting. It will lie flat if you bend the folds in the opposite direction.

11. <u>Mirror</u>---a full length mirror can be as little as a $10.00 investment and must be in your sewing area. If your sewing area is a corner of the living room, you might find or build a folding screen to hide it. If so, why not a mirrored screen?

12. A good steam iron ---we like the Sunbeam Shot-of-Steam or G.E. Surge of Steam. This type of iron makes sewing so much faster. Why? The extra jet of steam that makes that interfacing fuse faster and seams press flatter.

13. Extra machine bobbins---and a bobbin box grooved to hold them.

14. Paper lunch bag---tape to machine table to hold thread snips. We hate to clean house.

15. A mug rack---the handiest way we have found to store all grab-for type items. If they don't have holes large enough to slip over the mug pegs, attach a loop of colorful ribbon.

16. A pin cushion of some sort is almost essential---we especially like the wrist variety as it's always where you need it. A basic storage variety is also handy.

17. Bulletin board ---behind sewing machine holds pattern pieces, needles, pattern directions.

18. Pressing equipment -- see pressing chapter for more information.

19. Seam ripper---be honest, you'll need it. We aren't always perfect. We like the small one best, it's safer.

20. 7" - 8" bent handled shears (in good condition)---have you tried any of the new lightweights? They cut well and are VERY comfortable.

21. Embroidery scissors---don't skimp, get the best possible quality. Take fabric with you and make sure they cut all the way to the point on all fabrics you would normally sew. Use for clipping, snipping and trimming. Tie them to your machine for easy access.

22. 5" - 6" scissors---handy for light trimming and snipping.

KEEP YOUR SCISSORS FOR SEWING ONLY! Have them sharpened frequently and you will smile as you sew. How can you possibly cut an elegant blouse fabric with shears your husband used to replace the porch screens?

HONEY........I got the screen patched...
here's your scissors!

## THE TREATS

1. <u>See-Thru Ruler</u>---a handy clear plastic measuring aid great as a T-square for cutting and as a straight edge for marking.

2. <u>Talon® Basting Tape</u>---a double-faced sewing tape used in place of pins or hand basting, especially great for sewing zippers in stretchy knits.

3. <u>Magnetic seam gauge</u> **or** <u>masking tape</u>---placed a specified distance from the needle on the machine throat **plate**, it can be a nice guide for even sewing.

4. <u>Sobo Glue</u>---essential for speedy basting of interfacings and underlinings (unless using fusibles, of course).

5. <u>Pinking shears</u>---can be utilized in many ways besides finishing seams in ravelly fabrics. We'll show you how later.

6. <u>An organizer tray</u>---for small items you can't hold on your mug rack. Keep it close to your machine. If you can't find one in the fabric department, try an office supply or stationery store.

7. <u>Fray Check™ by Dritz</u>---A clear liquid used to prevent ravelling. Great for the corners of bound buttonholes and collar points.

8. <u>Steamstress by Osrow</u>---a super steamer for pressing as you sew. It even allows you to top press on velvet and Ultrasuede.

9. <u>Iron All®</u> --- an attachment that snaps onto the bottom of the iron and eliminates the need for a press cloth.

10. <u>Clean & Glide® by Stacy or iron-off™ by Dritz</u>---hot iron cleaners that are great for removing fusible web and other residue from bottom of iron.

11. <u>Cut and press board</u>---a fantastic time-saver. You can place this padded cutting and pressing board on a chest of drawers at elbow height next to your sewing machine. Advantages: you can steam and preshrink fabrics on it; block or straighten off-grain fabric; use the large surface for fusing interfacings in place; and press as you sew. See the illustration on page 13 of how it is used in Pati's sewing room - it actually replaces her ironing board. You can make your own board by purchasing a 36" by 54" piece of 5/8" thick pressed board. Put 1/2" thick layer of old wool Army blankets or Rayon and wool rug pad on top. Cover with heavy muslin stapled or masking taped to the back side. Do not use polyester batting as it's nonabsorbent. See pg. 106 for additional pressing equipment.

12. <u>Washable Marker™ by Fashionetics</u>---a super new marking pencil with washable "ink". Can even mark on right side of fabric. Just think - write notes to yourself on the fabric as you sew!

# A ~~FEW THOUGHTS~~ DISSERTATION ON THREAD

With so many different types of thread available today, confusion is understandable. We hope we can answer a few of your questions.

Polyester thread - the most all-purpose thread, since it can be used on any fabric. It doesn't shrink or fade and is the strongest of all the threads, so is ideal for hemming. You'll never have another hem thread break. Polyester thread also stretches, making it compatible with knits. There is definitely a difference in the quality of the many polyester threads on the market--a "bargain" thread may create many headaches. Look for a thread that is smooth, even, fine, and strong. Both all polyester or cotton-wrapped polyester threads are good. There are some beautiful new imported "long staple" polyester threads that have improved hand sewing ability, greater luster, and extra strength. Some have recently been developed in the United States also. 4 - 5 1/2" fibers are used in place of 1 1/2" fibers for spinning the threads. This produces a superiour quality thread that is practically tangle free. When hand sewing with synthetic threads, use a shorter than normal length to reduce static build-up and knotting and cut thread diagonally off the spool for easier needle threading. Coats & Clark makes an extra fine polyester thread for lingerie that is great for sewing light weight synthetics.

Cotton thread - a natural for cotton fabrics. Some disadvantages: cotton thread may shrink and is not recommended for low-shrink synthetic fabrics. Cotton thread is not as strong as polyester and synthetic fabrics can actually cut it like glass rubbing against tissue paper.

Silk thread - made from protein. It works well on protein fabrics like silk and wool. Silk thread is quite strong and elastic. It is so fine that we like it for delicate fabrics like silky Qiana.

Silk buttonhole twist - a heavy silk thread used for decorative topstitching. This is a fat thread and it needs a fat needle eye to pass through to keep it from shredding. Try a large

machine needle--size 16 or 18.  Different machines will sew
with silk buttonhole twist in different ways -- try all three
before you insist your machine refuses to sew with this thread:
1. The most common---twist on top, regular thread
   of any fiber content in the bobbin.
2. Regular thread on top, twist in the bobbin.
3. Twist on top and the bobbin.
Silk buttonhole twist will wash nicely, but some dark colors
may not be totally colorfast, especially navy, black and red.
If you are using a dark color on a light fabric, make a test
sample and launder it.  This elegant thread with its subtle
sheen is well worth the extra effort.

Polyester buttonhole twist  (also called polyester topstitching
thread) - a new thread that solves the color fade and shrinkage
problem of silk buttonhole twist.  Some brands are extremely
heavy and must be used with a size 18 needle.  New polyester
topstitching threads are being developed that even have a sheen
like silk.  Don't forget the Singer Yellow Band (#2045) needle.
It seems to work with these heavier threads in stopping skipped
stitches when all else fails.

Thread color
     Pati was a very frustrated buyer for a sewing notions depart-
ment when she found her customers always insisting upon "perfect"
thread match for every fabric.  We like to use matching threads
whenever possible, but we certainly don't drive to 76 stores nor
lose sleep over it if we can't match it perfectly.  Generally,
choose thread a shade darker as it will appear lighter off the
spool as it sews in.  If a perfect match for topstitching is not
possible, go a shade lighter for a dressier and more elegant
effect, a shade darker for a sportier look, or a complete contrast
for a very casual appearance.

# THE BIGGIE

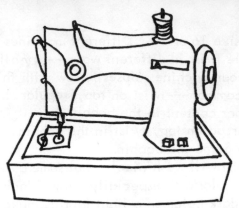

Investing in a sewing machine may be one of your larger expenditures, so take time to make the right choice. Machines are like people, they have individual personalities. Be sure to try several brands to see which suits you best. Some dealers have a home trial program and some "rent-with-option-to-buy." So do test--you wouldn't buy a car without a test drive, would you?

We would prefer to suggest a top-of-the-line machine in any brand, because it would do everything but sing to you. But, is it really the best choice for you? The woman who plans to do no more than patch jeans and make decorator pillows does not need that much machine. It would be like buying a Porsche and letting it sit in the garage.

One of our pet peeves is a beginning seamstress (or her husband) buying an $800 machine when she isn't even sure she wants to sew. Know your needs and budget and then shop to find out all the options available before making your choice. If the $800 machine is easier for you to operate, (and you need all the help you can get), then that alone might justify it. If you are really confused, consider the following guidelines. Are you...

1. A beginner -- have never sewed before, not sure if you'll even like it, but need something to sew on. Perhaps you should look for a very simple, sturdy, basic machine. Consider an $89.99 special or even a used machine. You can decide to trade for a more expensive model later or keep it for your children.

2. Someone who has been sewing for some time -- you really like your old machine, but want something new. Find a good basic zig-zag machine with a built-in buttonholer. You might want a stretch stitch if you frequently sew with knits. It also gives extra durability in seams in children's

clothes. A stretch stitch is not a necessity--but a convenience. Susan's mother has a 35 year old straight stitch machine that she uses for knits. We feel, however, that a zig-zag is almost a necessity today, especially with the return of woven fabrics. It is the easiest way to finish the edges of a ravelly fabric.

3.  You love to sew, sew constantly, try all the new patterns and fabrics and want the "ultimate" in a machine. Then perhaps you are the top-of-the-line customer. A mid-priced machine may have a stretch stitch, built-in button-holer, and zig-zag, but the "ultimate" has decorative stitches for fantastic embroidery. It will also usually have Pati's favorite stitch for armholes and pant crotches - the stretch-overlock stitch.

No matter what machine you buy, discipline yourself to learn to use it. Take any lessons the machine dealer offers. Insist on a complete set of instruction books with any new or used machine. But then practice!! Pati had to force herself to learn to use her buttonholer. She decided to sit for a half hour or until she completed 100 machine buttonholes, whichever came first. She now makes gorgeous speedy machine buttonholes! So try it!

Remember---you paid for all the gadgets on that machine, now use them! And keep the machine oiled, lint-free and in good working condition. Read your manual and follow the care instructions completely.

After the machine, selecting the cabinet becomes the next big task. The most important thing to look for is a large top working surface. Drawers are secondary - you can always buy an inexpensive chest for storage. Most new machines are portables that may be set into a table or cabinet of your choice. If space is a problem, there are some beautiful little lightweight folding tables available.

## WHERE TO BUY YOUR MACHINE

Selecting the right dealer is important. We have never heard of a dealer who will take back a machine because you "don't like it." This makes it all the more important, especially if you are buying an expensive machine, to find someone you like and can trust. Find one who offers lessons on the use of the machine and who can service it over the years.

## What's "BASIC" in a machine to make sewing painless?

1. A good even balanced straight stitch that goes forward and reverse.
2. A zig-zag stitch for stretch seams and finishing seams.
3. Built-in or attachment for machine buttonholes.

## What's classified as a "REALLY HELPFUL" addition?

1. Serpentine stitch to finish edges on lightweight ravelly fabrics.

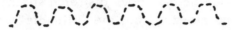

2. A blind hem stitch to make a nice invisible machine hem.

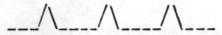

## What we feel are "NEAT LUXURIES".

1. A free-arm machine---good for sleeves and small items and patching knees in pants.

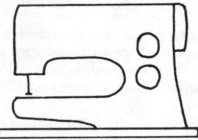

2. Stretch stitch---necessary only for stretch swim and ski wear, but nice for knits.

3. Stretch overlock stitches---for stitching seams and finishing at the same time. Nice for knits and super as a finish for crotch and armscye seams.

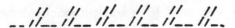

4. Needle positions---allows flexibility in stitch placement. Changing needle to left or right helps in topstitching.

# Quick Shaping

The entire concept of sewing shape into our clothes has changed through the years. Remember the 1960's when garments were related to buildings and we used inner construction that would hold up a skyscraper? A jacket could virtually stand up by itself! Today, thank goodness, clothes rely on subtle shaping. The old terminology is still with us, but the fabrics, the methods and the reasons for shaping have all changed.

## THE TERMS

Lining--a layer of fabric constructed separately from the garment. It is used to cover everything else that is inside.

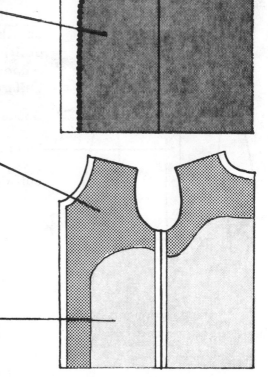

Interfacing--a layer of firm fabric placed along the edges of the fashion fabric to help them wear better and in details to give body, such as pockets and collars.

Underlining --a layer of fabric cut from the same pattern pieces as the fashion fabric, but the two are sewed together and treated as one in all seams.

## INTERFACINGS: Where to Use

Edges --- because edges are subject to excessive wear and
interfacings provide strength, body, and stretch
prevention in these areas.

Neckline needs help
because it supports the
entire garment.

Armscye needs help
because of perspiration
wear.

Front needs
help because
of the number
of times we
handle the edge
just in button-
ing.

collar detail

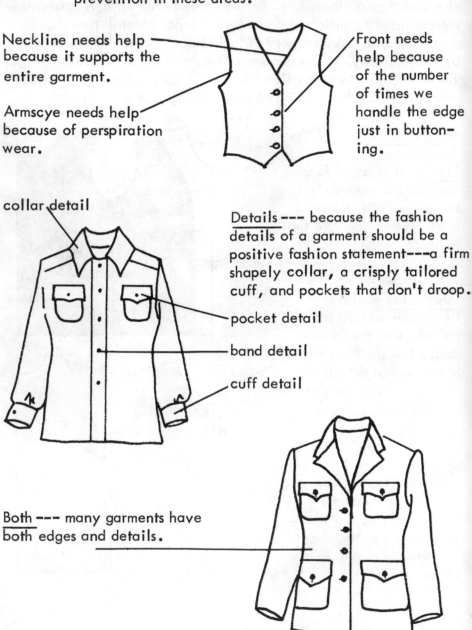

Details --- because the fashion
details of a garment should be a
positive fashion statement---a firm
shapely collar, a crisply tailored
cuff, and pockets that don't droop.

pocket detail

band detail

cuff detail

Both --- many garments have
both edges and details.

## HOW TO CHOOSE AN INTERFACING:

We recommend placing your fashion fabric on top of your interfacing and feeling the two together. Check the following:

1. Does the interfacing give your fabric enough or too much body?
2. Does the interfacing change the color of the fashion fabric?
3. Are the two fabrics compatible as far as care?
4. Try draping the two to a shape that resembles the place they will be used together. For example, fold them around your wrist to resemble a cuff.

NOTE: We can't generalize and say use heavy interfacings with heavy fabrics and light interfacings with light fabrics. A light fabric may need the body of a heavier interfacing in some detail areas, and a heavy fabric may just need a tiny bit of help from a light weight interfacing to prevent stretch. If in doubt, make a test sample to check for the right inter-facing needed.

## OTHER FACTORS TO CONSIDER WHEN SELECTING AN INTERFACING

1. If the garment is a glamorous evening frock that you plan to wear once, interface for look only -- durability will not be a factor.
2. Different garments get different amounts of strain. We would interface the hem of a coat because it gets a tremendous amount of strain, but not a dress hem unless you want it to look soft and rolled or to stand out.
3. Fabric plays a very important part. Even a soft drapey look may need an interfacing to prevent a soft droopy look.

4. When in doubt interface. Our experience has proved to us that most things can look terrific when they are brand new, but interfaced things still look great years later. Garments without interfacings develop the "saggies" much faster.
5. When in doubt, ask the saleslady. We all like our clothing to fit and feel differently, but remember, if you really love soft sensuous things and the saleslady is wearing a structured linen dress, trust your own sense of touch, not hers.
6. No matter what interfacing you use, it will probably look better than if you used nothing.

## FUSIBLES VS. STITCHABLES

| FUSIBLES | STITCHABLES |
|---|---|
| We suggest fusible interfacings wherever possible. They give the best look in the least time and least amount of hassle, even for the inexperienced. They are especially nice with knit fabrics and they are an outstanding help in any area you plan to topstitch. They firm up the area so your topstitching is smooth. | Even though we highly recommend fusible interfacings, there is still a place in fine sewing for stitchables. Because a fusible becomes somewhat firmer after application, a stitchable may give you a softer more subtle shape and can be used with all fabrics. |

NOTE: Fusibles get firmer after fusing. For example, the filler is left out of Fusible Acro, so it is soft when purchased, but will get firmer after fusing.

### DO YOU HATE TO BASTE?
From now on think of the stitchables as the GLUEABLES. We will show you how to elimate pinning and basting by using glue.

NOTE: Stitchables get softer after use, especially washing.

| WHERE TO USE FUSIBLES | WHERE TO USE STITCHABLES |
|---|---|
| Woven fusible interfacings work well with woven fabrics. Non-woven fusible interfacings work well with knits. If in doubt--make a test sample.<br><br>Even though we say fusibles can't be used on napped fabrics, there are EXCEPTIONS to every rule. Ultrasuede, a napped fabric, fuses beautifully. Pati loves fusible Feather-weight Pellon on some sheer fabrics,and even some corduroys may be fused if a terry towel is used under the face to cushion the nap. IF IN DOUBT--TEST!! | Woven stitchables are good with both woven and knit fabrics. Non-woven stitchables may "buckle" in an enclosed area. They can't contract as well as wovens, yet they can expand and give with knits.<br><br>Stitchables are recommended in some fabrics because fusibles:<br>... flatten gauze and seersucker<br>... may not adhere such as to triacetate<br>... may ruin fabrics that can't tolerate steam (some silks and Chinon)<br>... may flatten the nap of some roy or velvets. |

| PRESHRINKING FUSIBLES | PRESHRINKING STITCHABLES |
|---|---|
| Woven fusibles--place in a basin of HOT water (it will not hurt the fusing agent which is only activated at 300 degrees or more) and soak for 10 minutes. Blot in a towel and hangar dry. DO NOT WAD UP AND WRING DRY. DO NOT THROW INTO DRYER. (The agitation dislodges the fusing agent.)<br>Non-woven fusibles --no need to preshrink.<br>Fusible web--NO NO NO NO---do not preshrink. | Most woven stitchables inter-facings have a small shrinkage factor and it is best to preshrink to assure compatibility with the fashion fabric. Preshrink as you plan to wash the finished garment. Be sure to use detergent.<br>Non-woven stitchables are basically shrinkage free. |

## HOW TO FUSE

OK, we have convinced you to try a fusible. Now, how does this stuff work? Most products will come with very specific instructions on fusing techniques. Read and carefully follow manufacturer's instructions. BE SURE TO NOTICE:

1. If instructions suggest steam or dry iron.
2. The number of seconds heat must be applied.
3. If a press cloth is necessary (does it say damp or dry).
4. If there are fabrics or uses that should be avoided.

If the fusible you have has no instructions with it, there are some GENERAL PROCEDURES you can follow to insure maxium success.

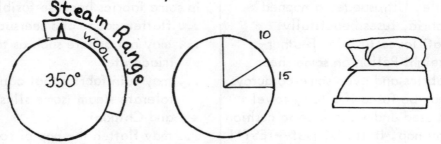

1. Preheat iron, set on "WOOL" setting.
2. Fuse for 10-15 seconds per section without sliding iron.
3. Use firm, two-handed pressure.
4. Not all manufacturers recommend a press cloth, but we prefer one. It saves getting residue on the bottom of your iron--the see-through variety is best.

## TO FUSE OR NOT TO FUSE ---THAT IS THE QUESTION!!

The new fusibles aren't really the same as the old iron-ons or bake-on interfacings. Iron-ons had a polyethylene resin (plastic bag material) in the form of flake-off granules on the back side. You used a dry hot iron to get them to adhere until after the first wash.

Today's fusibles rely on new polyethelene and polyamide resins that are fused with steam. The new resins are applied to the interfacings in new methods such as the computer-dot or the calendaring method, they don't flake off as easily.

42

## SOME FUSING SUGGESTIONS

1. Be patient. Always allow fused pieces to cool before moving.
2. Cheat. You don't have to trim away 1/2" of the interfacing seam allowance on medium and light weight fabrics as long as you carefully grade or layer seams when trimming. Try a quick test sample to see how bulky the seam will be.
3. Use a minimum of 10 seconds to fuse any fabric. The heavier the fabric, the more seconds you should use. Susan uses the MISSISSIPPI trick. One Mississippi, two Mississippi, three Mississippi, etc. You will then be sure to count 15 seconds.

NOTE: How to unfuse. Steam press the area for 5 seconds, pulling apart while still hot. Any excess resin can generally be absorbed by pressing the area with a damp press cloth. If fusing agent comes in contact with the sole plate of the iron, remove with a commercial hot iron cleaner (available in sewing notion departments) or a mild abrasive.

## STEAM SHRINKING --- A NEW CONCEPT FOR FUSIBLES

This is a new thought from Pati. We have found that steam may cause the interfacing and the fashion fabric to shrink more than it did by being simply washed, due to the excessive heat. Try this step-by-step method when fusing a fusible interfacing in place:

1. "Warm" your fashion fabric by pressing with steam. This removes wrinkles and any remaining shrinkage.
2. Place your interfacing on your fabric (resin side down)
3. Hold your iron 1" - 2" above the interfacing and steam for 5 seconds. (A Shot-of-Steam type iron is a great help--it does a better job and is faster). You will actually see some of the interfacings shrink up (especially some non-wovens).
4. Now FUSE the two together.

## STEAM BASTING

This is a quick way to control your fusible interfacing. Lightly press from the centers to outside edges for 1 second in each spot. This keeps it from slipping while fusing.

## HOW TO GLUE

Basting an interfacing in place is tedious and not always accurate. There is too much chance for the interfacing to slip while sewing.

What is the answer? --- GLUING!

With What? --- SOBO GLUE! Sobo is a fabric glue that dries fairly clear and soft. It can be found in most sewing notion departments.

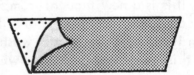

Where do you glue? ---On the very edge of the seam allowance using small dots of Sobo.

1. Press the two layers together.

2. Dot glue on seam allowances and pat together.

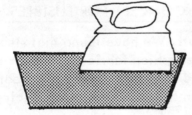

3. Treat collar/glued interfacing layer as one.

It takes 5 minutes to dry. It will NOT WASH OUT, so only get it on the very edges.

See page 50 for gluing tips for underlining.

# WHERE TO INTERFACE --- THE SPECIFICS

|  | FUSIBLES | STITCHABLES (GLUEABLES) |
|---|---|---|

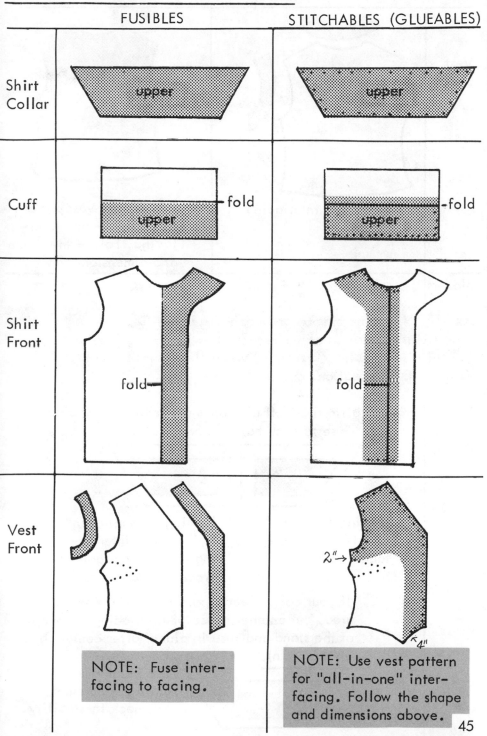

**Shirt Collar** — upper / upper

**Cuff** — fold / upper — -fold / upper

**Shirt Front** — fold / fold

**Vest Front** — 2" / 4"

NOTE: Fuse inter-facing to facing.

NOTE: Use vest pattern for "all-in-one" inter-facing. Follow the shape and dimensions above.

45

|  |  |  |
|---|---|---|
| **Vest Back** |  | 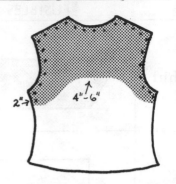 |
|  | NOTE: Fuse interfacing to facing. | NOTE: Use vest pattern for "all-in-one" inter-facing. Follow the shape and dimensions above. |

**Blazers**

NOTE: We think blazers and coats are beautiful, but they are definitely not painless, especially when custom tailor-ing with stitchables. Therefore, we will only talk about fusibles in this section.

**Blazer Under Collar**

1. Trim 1/2" off all edges of fusible interfacing. Fuse to each half of under collar.

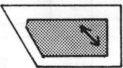 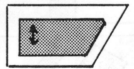

If using a "woven" fusible, cut inter-facing on bias.

If using a "nonwoven" fusible, cut interfac-ing with stretch going around neck.

2. If your collar needs extra body in the stand area, cut another piece of interfacing the shape of the stand and fuse in place (after center back seam is sewn).

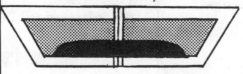

The lengthwise grain goes around the neck for stability.

Blazer Upper Collar---Glue underlining to wrong side for extra body and to cushion seams. Follow stitchable shirt upper collar directions on page 45.   Optional in heavy knits.

Blazer Back --- Use lightweight stitchable interfacing and cut same as "stitchable" vest back.

## BLAZER FRONT -- 4 METHODS

1. Fuse to facing and lapel only. Trim 1/2" off interfacing.

2. Fuse to entire front. Trim 1/2" from interfacing. May fuse double layer in lapel.

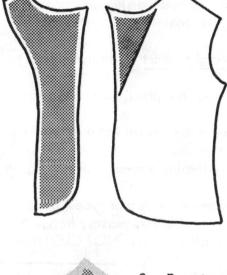

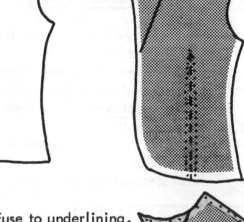

3. Fuse to underlining.
   (a) Trim 3/4" from interfacing. Fuse to underlining. Mark darts on underlining, <u>cut out</u> of interfacing.

   (b) Glue unit to fashion fabric. Sew darts through all layers.

4. (not shown) Fuse to fashion fabric. Use pattern for interfacing, trim away 1/2".

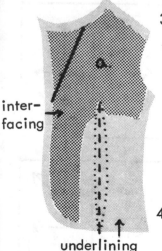

inter-facing

underlining

47

# WHAT DO WE MEAN BY "GIVE" IN INTERFACINGS?

The new interfacings have give in at least one direction. Woven interfacings have always had bias give, but old fashioned non-wovens had no give and were stiff and boardy. Today's interfacings are more flexible because of the "give" they have.

Use "give" to your advantage:
1. The direction that gives creates comfort, soft supple rolls in collars, and more subtle shaping in knits.
2. Stable directions prevent give or stretch in buttonholes, add firm body in front bands and waistbands, and prevent pockets from stretching.

Types of Give (See Interfacing Weight Chart for brand names.)

1. Bias -- Woven fabrics have lengthwise and crosswise stability and bias give.
2. Crosswise -- Some new non-wovens have lengthwise stability and crosswise stretch.
3. Multi-directional -- All-bias non-wovens have give in all directions.
4. No Give -- Some non-wovens (older types) have no give. They are best used for belts, purses, hats, home decorating, and craft projects, NOT CLOTHING!

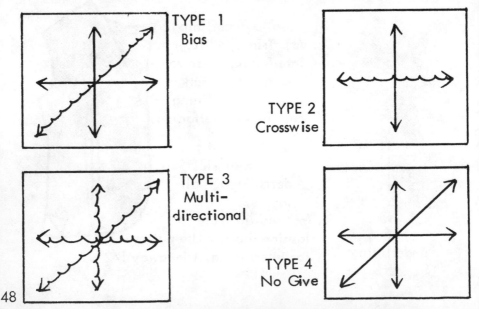

TYPE 1
Bias

TYPE 2
Crosswise

TYPE 3
Multi-directional

TYPE 4
No Give

## WHICH ONES

### HELP! "THERE ARE TOO MANY INTERFACINGS AND I'M CONFUSED."

We hear this all the time, and rightfully so. But don't let interfacing selection become a big deal. Trust us! Interfacings today are simple to use and we can expect super performance from many of them. We have catagorized a few of the brand names we like in an INTERFACING WEIGHT CHART to help you get started. We have chosen a few from each of the major manufacturers that you can stock at home. We think serious seamstresses should have their own interfacing "STORE" at home. Buy a yard of each of your favorites, preshrink, label, and put in a drawer or file in shoe boxes. They are now ready to use --- even if you decide to use three different interfacings in one garment. You'd never do that without your own "store"!

### INTERFACING WEIGHT CHART
Type of Give in Parentheses

|  | STITCHABLE | FUSIBLE |
|---|---|---|
| Light Weight | Sta-Shape (1)<br>Armo-Press (1) | Fusible Featherweight Pellon (3)<br>Sheer-weight fusible Pellon (3)<br>Lightweight Easy-Shaper (2)<br>Sof-Shape® by Pellon (2)<br>Shape Flex (1) |
| Medium Weight | Veriform Durable Press (1) | Midweight Fusible Pellon (2)<br>Shape-Flex (1)<br>Suit Weight Easy Shaper (2)<br>Armo-Weft (1)<br>Shirt-Fuse™ (2)<br>Mediumweight Pel-Aire (2) |
| Heavy Weight | Acro (1) | Fusible Acro (1)<br>Heavyweight Pel-Aire (2) |

## UNDERLINING

We feel underlining is next in importance to interfacing.

### Where is an underlining used?

1. In the body of a sheer fabric to prevent lingerie and seam allowances from shadowing through.
2. In pants to prevent baggy knees and fanny.
3. For a truly invisible hem in any garment.
4. In woven fabrics more often than knits, expecially if loosely woven as they will wear longer.

### What is used?

1. For a small amount of body -- Poly-SiBonne or polyester linin
2. For more body -- Keynote Plus    (lightweight cotton/poly)
3. For even more body -- Veriform Durable Press
4. For even more body -- Fuse-A-Knit or Easy Knit

Choose the underlining fabric by the amount of body you need to give your fashion fabric the look you want.

NOTE: If you decide you have to underline, have some fun with it. If yellow is your favorite color, but it really makes you look jaundiced, UNDERLINE with yellow! If you harbor a secret desire to feel like Samantha the Siren - underline with RED!

### Underlining is easy -- if you GLUE!

1. Sobo glue is the fabric glue we used in the stitchable (glueable) interfacing section. It also makes under-linings "glueable." Caution: it is permanent when dry. Use glue in seam allowances, close to edge of fabric only.
2. Simply place your fabric on a flat padded pressing surface. Steam press all the wrinkles out.

3. Place your underlining on top and press the two together.
   This removes wrinkles and any excess shrinkage caused by
   steam. Lift underlining and dot Sobo glue on fashion fabric
   close to the edge in seam allowances. Pat the two layers
   together. Allow 5 minutes to dry.

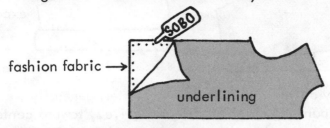

fashion fabric →

underlining

## The "Glue and Fold" Technique

When a garment is on your body, it is not on a flat surface
like it is when on the table. When on your body, these two
layers go around a cylinder. If they are glued together on a flat
surface, they will look like this when on the body:

With the "glue and fold" method, we make the inside cylinder
slightly smaller like this:

Here's how:
1. After gluing the two layers together, fold them in half
   lengthwise. You will see a bubble in the underlining. Scoot
   it off the opposite side by smoothing with your hand while
   the glue is still wet.

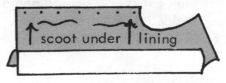

scoot under lining

2. As a "very general" rule of thumb, we fold once for every seam allowance that gets pressed in. Fold each pant leg two times. Fold each sleeve twice. Fold each skirt piece twice

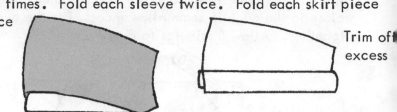

Trim off excess

3. Which way do you fold? It doesn't matter; generally we fold each pant leg the same direction, i.e., toward center.
4. Check yourself...Have I scooted too much? Wait until the glue is dry. If you hold the two layers up straight the fashion fabric will be larger.

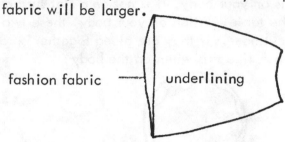

fashion fabric ———— underlining

5. You can "quick check" to see if it is too large by taking the garment and folding in the seam allowances as if they had been pressed and sewed and curving the section into a half moon. Does the curve use up all the excess?

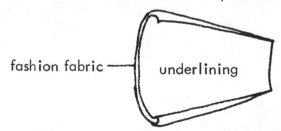

fashion fabric ——— underlining

6. How do you unglue? Reheat the glue dots with an iron for 3 seconds and gently pull apart.

NOTE: How to get glue out if you goofed and didn't follow instructions and glued inside the seam allowance. YOU DON'T! WE HAVE TRIED EVERYTHING. PLEASE...be careful!

## Exceptions

1. Where you are flat and there are no seam allowances pressed in, don't fold at all. For example, across the upper back or chest of a garment with sleeves there is no need to fold because the sleeve seam allowance goes into the sleeve.
2. It would be difficult to fold twice below the armscye if you aren't folding at all above, so just fold once even if there are two seam allowances.
3. Any garment with small vertical sections, once is enough. Each gore in an eight gored skirt or an eight gored blazer is pretty narrow. Fold once only.

4. If a collar or yoke is interfaced, fold horizontally once.

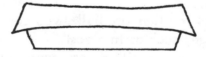

## OTHER POINTS

1. There is no need to trim off the excess underlining unless it gets in your way. Actually, it is best to leave it as an extra cushion for the seams.
2. Susan separates the underlining and fashion fabric when she is ready to press the seams open by running her finger between them the length of the seam. She feels this makes her seams press more smoothly.
3. Do not glue a hem together as the underlining must be free to slip when you press the hem up (another inner cylinder).
4. If darts are marked on underlining and they move noticeably, you may adjust them.

# LINING

Lining is always a time consuming adventure because it means we cut and sew two separate garments and then sew those two together. Double effort. Therefore, we try to avoid lining.

## WHEN IS IT POSSIBLE TO AVOID LINING

1. When you underline a skirt or pants or dress. All you get is another layer, and it hides your pretty red underlining.
2. When your fabric has enough body to look great without anything.
3. When you want to look slinky in a slinky fabric. (Unless you want the dress to "slink past" a few extra bulges.)

## WHEN IS IT IMPOSSIBLE TO IGNORE LINING

1. In a nice coat or blazer that would slip on and off better if it had a slippery lining inside.
2. When you really want to hide the inner construction, as in a coat or blazer.

NOTE: Many times an "unlined" blazer is harder to make because you have to figure out how to finish the seams so they look nice.

3. When you need extra warmth.
4. When you are working with a see-through fabric that you don't want to see through and where an underlining would not be suitable.
5. When you want to eliminate bulk, you can line a garment to the edge, such as in a vest.
6. When you are working with a very expensive fabric and lining to the edge would save you $$$.

## WHAT DO YOU USE

We find that the best thing to use for a lining that will wear forever and won't droop or split is a lightweight polyester. We like Ciao, AlaCreme, Butterfly, and Coupe De Ville. If you can find a light weight printed polyester fabric, use it for a "fun" lining.

NOTE: A print lining with a matching print dress or blouse is a very classy touch. If wearing a print-lined jacket over a different print blouse offends you, look for some of the inoffensive and insignificant prints that really blend with anything. Stripes, dots, checks, and small two-color prints are very versatile. Think about it this way: If Pierre Cardin can put a loud (but gorgeous) red plaid lining inside a conservative grey flannel suit, we can use a dot or stripe.

## LINING A SKIRT

1. Make the skirt in your fashion fabric.

2. Make the skirt in the lining fabric.

3. Attach the two right sides together at the waist.

4. Attach waistband and finish lining around zipper by hand slip stitching.

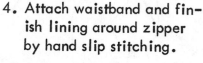

## FINISHING A HEM IN A LINING

1. The lining should always be cut to the length of the finished garment. When turned up it will ALWAYS be shorter than the garment and not show.

2. A "jump hem" is a tidy way to finish any lined garment. Hem the garment first, then press under the lining to the desired length and pin about one inch away from pressed edge. Fold back the pressed edge at pins and stitch lining to garment hem with a long hemming stitch. Be sure to catch only the lining hem allowance and not the lining itself.

(inside garment)
lining

Flip lining -- A completely machine sewed vest.

1. Make lining small-
er by trimming 1/8"
from neck, armscyes, and
front. (This keeps lining
from showing when vest
is finished.)

1/8" off  1/8" off  1/8" off

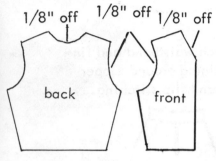

2. Sew darts and should-
er seams in both lining
and fashion fabric.

lining

fashion fabric

3. Match lining to fashion fabric
right sides together at neck, armholes and front. Stitch using small
stitches at curves and corners.

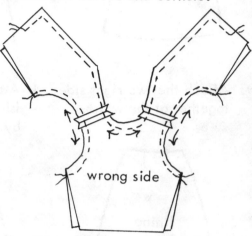

4. Trim, grade, and press the
seams you have just sewed. Also
clip, notch, and slash where
necessary. (See page 94.)

5. Turn vest to right side by
reaching through back shoulders
and pulling vest fronts through.

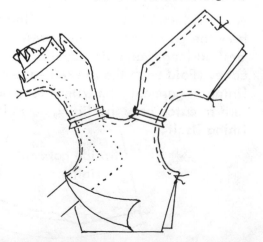

8. Stitch across bottom. Leave a 5" opening. Trim seam.

HINT: Machine baste across 5" opening. Snip basting thread to form opening.

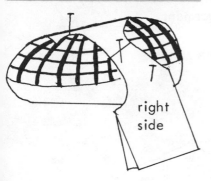

right side

wrong side

5"

9. Turn vest through the 5" opening and press bottom edge. Slip stitch the opening closed.

6. Sew side seams by matching underarm seams. Sew lining front and back right sides together and fashion fabric front and back right sides together at side seams. Press side seams open.

7. After side seams are stitched, turn wrong side out through opening at bottom.

opening

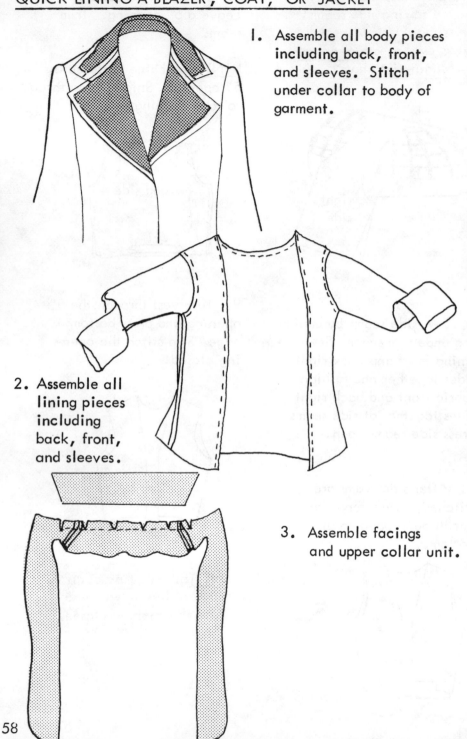

1. Assemble all body pieces including back, front, and sleeves. Stitch under collar to body of garment.

2. Assemble all lining pieces including back, front, and sleeves.

3. Assemble facings and upper collar unit.

58

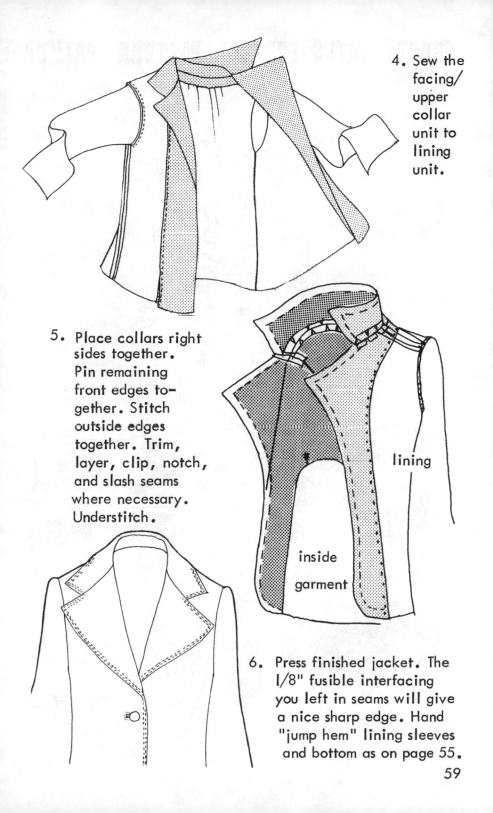

4. Sew the facing/ upper collar unit to lining unit.

5. Place collars right sides together. Pin remaining front edges together. Stitch outside edges together. Trim, layer, clip, notch, and slash seams where necessary. Understitch.

lining

inside

garment

6. Press finished jacket. The 1/8" fusible interfacing you left in seams will give a nice sharp edge. Hand "jump hem" lining sleeves and bottom as on page 55.

59

"I'll just make it fit!"

# PRETTY PATI'S PERFECT PATTERN PRIMER

We chose this wording for the sake of alliteration, but we were serious about the importance of emphasizing good fit as a part of good sewing.

Some people we have talked to are not aware of what good fit is --- for various reasons. One said it had been so long since she was able to buy something that fit well that she'd just forgotten what it was like. Another said that with all the new fashion looks --- it is confusing to know what "good" fit is.

The standards of good fit do change with fashion and as full as fashion sometimes is---you wonder if you need to know "anything" about fit. However, we are seeing a return to the fitted look. Yves St. Laurent brought out his "Siren" look in early 1975 (also called the "Tube"). This was the first hint of the trend toward closer more feminine clothing. Skirts, dresses and pant legs are now slimmer, making fit more important again.

## STANDARDS OF GOOD FIT
1. The garment is neither too tight nor too loose.
2. The crosswise grain at bust and hip is parallel with the floor.
3. The side seams are perpendicular to floor and in center of leg.
4. The shoulder seams are in center of shoulders.
5. The top of the set in sleeve is right at the pivot bone.
6. There are no wrinkles "pointing to problems."

## WHAT DO WE MEAN BY A PERFECT PATTERN?

### There isn't one!!!!!!

Even if a pattern is close to your size and shape as most altered "basic" patterns are, it is still not going to be "perfect." In other words you cannot expect to take your pattern, lay it on your fabric, cut it out, sew it up, and wear it without ever trying it on and expect a perfect fit. There are far too many VARIABLES.

# THE VARIABLES

1. Pati says that if she'd stop eating, she'd quickly eliminate one variable -- <u>fluctuation in weight</u>. SOLUTION: make sure every pattern you sew is large enough. In addition, to be safe---allow 1" side seam allowances. You can then take the side seams in or let them out, depending on how much you fluxuate between the time you cut the pattern out and the time you sew it up.

2. <u>Cutting</u> is the second variable. Have you ever cut out your fashion fabric, then used the same pattern piece for your underlining---and the two don't match exactly? All fabrics cut differently---they may slip or it may be due to the weight of the fabric. If you make an 1/8" error in cutting an 8 gore skirt, that means your skirt would be 2" too large OR 2" too small!! SOLUTION: make every pattern large enough that you won't have to worry.

3. <u>Fabric</u>, of course, is a variable in itself. Every fabric hangs differently on your body and requires a different amount of ease. Heavy fabrics need more room than light fabrics. Knits take less than wovens as they "give" as we move. We usually, for example, make knit pants 1" larger than our hips, but wovens are made 2" larger.

## EASE---WHAT IS IT AND HOW MUCH DO PATTERNS ALLOW?

The amount of ease depends on your posture and figure type. In Pati's pant fitting seminar, she asks everyone to stand and pinch out all the ease in their pants to one side.

If you can pinch 1" that is 2" ease

If you can pinch 1/2" that is 1" ease

If you can't pinch anything---help!

Only you can determine the amount of ease that is comfortable for you to wear. SOLUTION: add enough ease to the sides so that you can adjust garment ease to your liking when you are fitting as you sew. There are basically three types of ease allowances in a pattern.

### COMFORT EASE
Amount agreed upon by all pattern companies that is comfortable for most individuals.

### DESIGN EASE
A designer for a pattern company may decide to change the ease in order to achieve a special look.

### NO EASE
Really a FABRIC RE-QUIREMENT ease type. Some patterns allow little or no ease for very stretchy knits or even minus ease in bathing suits designed to stretch to fit.

### EASE VARIES WITH GARMENT TYPE

|  | Bust | Hip | Sleeve |
|---|---|---|---|
| Swimsuits | 0 | 0 | |
| Dress | 2 1/2" | 2 1/2" | 2 1/2" |
| Jacket | 4" | 4" | 4 1/2" |
| Coat* | 5" | 5" | 5 1/2" |

*Ease varies depending on what garment is to be worn over.

Another place the amount of ease varies is across the back 4" down from base of neck. You'll need 1/2" for a sleeveless garment, 1" for a garment with set-in-sleeves; and 1 1/2" for a coat.

## A VERY IMPORTANT POINT

A very good article in Vogue Pattern Magazine, May/June 1974 called "Facts About Fit" gives an explanation of how Vogue determines the amount of ease they allow in their patterns. They alert us that "the Vogue Pattern envelope illustration shows how the garment is meant to be worn...." For example, "the wearing ease for coats and jackets is determined by what is worn underneath....When buying a coat pattern, some consumers will automatically choose the next larger size, but this is not necessary...

Our coats are de-signed to fit over a blouse and a jacket." They also say that if you are not sure whether a coat truly can be worn over a jacket, read the caption. It will say, "Coat cannot be worn over jac-ket," if it truly can't be.

THE FOLLOWING EASE CHANGES HAVE RECENTLY BEEN MADE IN PATTERNS. THIS IS <u>NOT</u> THE SAME AS THE NEW SIZING WE HAD YEARS AGO.

1. The bustline has been lowered 5/8" (for most people this is fantastic---but for an unfortunate few of us--we'll have to raise our bust darts). This came about as a result of our bra-less and soft bra society.

2. Patterns were allowing 3" ease in the bust area for all sizes.
   Now:          sizes 6, 8, 10, 12          2 1/2" ease
                      14                      2 5/8"
                      16                      2 3/4"
                      18                      2 7/8"
                      20                      3"

3. Waistline ease allowance is now 1" (was 3/4")

4. Hip ease is now 2 1/2" (was 2")
   (Are we getting more pear shaped???)

5. Back waist length is now 5/8" longer for all sizes. This is mainly for a more rounded back--it is not the total waist length as front and back side seam lengths are still the same.

## THE TYPE OF PATTERN YOU BUY WILL BE YOUR CLUE TO THE WAY THE DESIGNER HAS ALTERED THE STANDARD EASE.

| Regular Patterns | Recommended for Knits | For Knits Only |
|---|---|---|
| Safely made from woven fabrics or knits with little stretch like poly-ester double knits. | Same as a regular pattern. Knits are mentioned to help sell the pattern. Also called "Suitable for Knits." | These are for knits that have lots of stretch. Some or all ease is removed. Use knit gauge on envelope. |

NOTE: Not only will a "Knits Only" pattern have less ease than a normal pattern, but often it will not have darts. If you are extremely full busted, you may have to avoid these patterns entirely or find a "Knits Only" pattern with darts.

## BUYING A PATTERN

Guides to selecting the correct size:
1. Buy a pant or skirt pattern by the hip size.

2. Buy a blouse pattern by the bust size.

NOTE: We recently designed two patterns for Vogue on fit: #1798 and # 2098. We learned some amazing things in the process. For example, if you are between sizes generally go to the smaller size as enough ease is allowed until you actually reach that next measurement.

NOTE: We learned something else – patterns are made for size B bra cup. If you are larger – you may be purchasing too large a pattern when you really just need extra in the bust. Therefore, take your bust and high bust measurements (taken high up under your arms and above the bust.) If there is 2 1/2" or more difference, buy pattern by the high bust. I.e. if you're a 10 high bust and a 14 full bust, buy the 10 and make a bust enlargement alteration on the pattern (pg. 81). Vogue #2098 makes it easy because we included five pattern fronts – one for every bra cup size.

REMEMBER ----- every size 10 WILL FIT DIFFERENTLY! Every designer allows a different amount of ease for different looks. AND THAT IS FASHION ---- and we LIKE it! (Even though we have to make a few quick checks to make sure the pattern is at least large enough.)

First, we must remind you to remember the variables -- weight fluctuation, cutting error, and fabric weight. So please don't blame the patterns for improper fit. Also--try to forget the following when selecting a pattern: "Vogue is too complicated;" "McCalls runs large;" and "Vogue is for the tall and slim," etc. If you think this way, you are only limiting yourself. It takes all the fun out of sewing. Pattern companies are constantly changing their own staff of designers and changing technically --- so be open minded and LEARN TO FIT AS YOU SEW!

## HOW TO FLAT PATTERN MEASURE

1. Always check your problem areas. Measure the pattern in those areas.
2. The horizontal measurements are the most important. It is more important that the blouse button in front than that the length is a bit short. (Of course, it would be ideal to get both correct.)
3. Always take the pattern measurement the same place on the pattern as you did on the body.

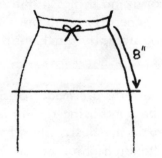 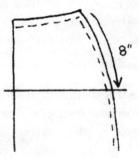

4. Include NO seam allowances or darts when you measure.

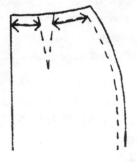

For "quickie" measuring, measure from side seam to dart, pick up tape and measure from other side of dart to side seam. Pick up tape and begin on next pattern piece in same manner.

5. If measuring around a curve, stand the tape on edge.

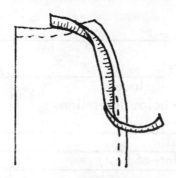

## BODY AND FLAT PATTERN MEASUREMENT CHART--USE PENCIL

1. Measure over undergarments only.
2. Fill in chart with pencil in case you change.
3. Pull tape snugly enough so it can't be moved.
4. Tie 1/4" elastic around waist. THE BOTTOM of the elastic is your waist.
5. If you use a heavy fabric, you may need to subtract 1/4" from the shoulder to waist and shoulder to apex measurements. Heavy fabrics tend to drop more.

Front

Back

# BODY MEASUREMENTS

| WIDTH MEASUREMENTS | you | + ease = | amount needed |
|---|---|---|---|
| 1. High bust or chest (includes shoulder blades – helps determine pattern size) | | | |
| 2. Regular or full bust | | 2-3" | |
| 3. Apex to apex (points of bust) | | | |
| 4. Waist | | 1/2-1" | |
| 5. High hip 3" down from waist | | | |
| 6. Fullest part of hip NOTE: how far is this from waist | | 2" | |
| 7. Shoulder width | | | |
| 8. Across back shoulders 4" down from neck bone | | 1/4" | |
| 9. Upper arm at fullest part | | 2 1/2" | |

| LENGTH MEASUREMENTS | you | + ease = | amount needed |
|---|---|---|---|
| 1. Length from center of shoulder to apex | | | |
| 2. Length from center of shoulder to waist (straight down from bust) | | 1/4" | |
| 3. Sleeve length from pivot bone in shoulder to middle of wrist bone | | | |
| 4. Back waist length | | 1/4" | |
| 5. Dress length from back neck bone to hem | | | |
| 6. Skirt length from waist to hem at side | | | |

INDIVIDUAL PROBLEM IF NOTICEABLE: round shoulders_____
square or sloping shoulders_____ broad or narrow shoulders_____
sway back_____ high hip on one side_____ other_____

# WIDTH AND LENGTH MEASUREMENTS

| MEASURE PATTERN | ALTER LENGTH | ALTER WIDTH |
|---|---|---|

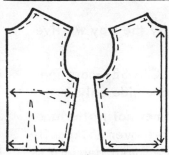 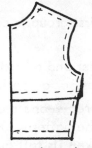 

Measure bust
and waist seam
to seam (not darts)

Shorten by tak-
ing tuck.
Do same to front
and back. Length-
en by spreading.

Add width from
armhole down.
Do same to front
and back. Pivot in
to make smaller.

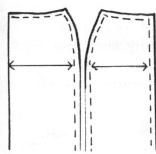 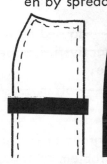 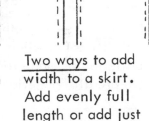

Measure hip at
fullest part from
side seam to side
seam.

Lengthen by spread-
ing pattern. Do same
to front and back.
Shorten with a tuck.

Two ways to add
width to a skirt.
Add evenly full
length or add just
to waist.

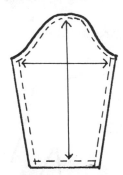 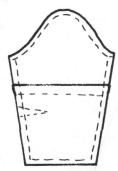 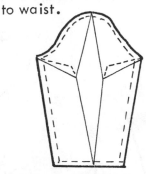

Measure across
underarm area and
from top to bottom.

Lengthen or short-
en above or be-
low elbow.

Cut on grainlines
and spread desir-
ed amount.

69

# TWO TYPES OF FITTING PROBLEMS

There are only a few really common fitting problems.

GRAVITY -- The first group is caused by the way we live and gravity.

1. A low shoulder and a high hip. CAUSE--carrying books, babies, or groceries on one side only.

2. A flat derriere ---one that is somewhat flatter and lower than the pattern. If you are over 25, gravity may have taken its toll and caused your derriere to drop.

3. A lower bustline --- it dropped, too. Not just due to to the fact that a more mature bust is often larger -- but it is also due to the no-bra or soft bra look. (And gravity?)

4. Round shoulders---caused by lots of reading and other sedentary activities, especially when done with poor posture.

5. Developed arms --- often caused by playing tennis or swimming.

GENETIC -- The other group of fitting problems is genetic and it's not really a "problem." It just so happens that patterns are made for the so-called average person and we are all "genetically" different.

The following are examples of common "genetic" fitting problems.

1. Sloping shoulders          2. Square shoulders

3. The curvature of waist and hipline (includes rib cage).

4. The length of different body sections (torso, pelvic, and legs). Five people standing in a row may all be the same height, but vary in waist and leg length.

"....but we're all 5'4" and wear a size 12!"

NOTE: Proportioned patterns are not necessarily the "answer" for a tall or short person. It depends on which part of you is tall or short. It is more important that you know where you are tall or short and buy a regular pattern and lengthen or shorten it in the right place.

## SO WHAT ARE MY FITTING PROBLEMS???

" Figure variations" are only problems if they CAUSE a problem in the clothes you wear. If there is no noticeable problem in the way things hang --- don't worry about it.

You will never know your fitting problems unless you KNOW YOUR BODY. Here are a few hints to help you get to know your own body better:

...BE HONEST...Cheating now is like cheating at solitare!

...GET A FULL LENGTH MIRROR. Do you own one now ?

___ If yes, you get 5 points .

___ If it is in your sewing area you get 10 points.

...ANALYZE your figure in front of your mirror. Do you have any of the following problems:

- a low shoulder on one side

- a high hip on one side

- a rounded back

- a flat and/or low derriere

## "BUT I'M ALL ALONE---HOW DO I FIT MYSELF?"

1. Take a SEWING CLASS and let the teacher do it for you.

2. MEASURE YOUR BODY and measure your pattern in the same places. Compare the two.

>ADVANTAGES: It is easy to do alone.
>DISADVANTAGES: It is hard to take accurate body measurements or to know how much ease to add.
>SOLUTION: Add more than enough ease to be safe.

3.  MAKE A MUSLIN.   This is a way to test a pattern before cutting into your fabric.
    > ADVANTAGES:  Gives you a good idea of how it will fit, how to sew it, and how it will look.
    > DISADVANTAGES: Costly.  Time consuming. Muslin may not hang like your fabric. Muslins are UGLY!

4.  FIT AS YOU SEW.
    > ADVANTAGES:  A fast way to get a good fit.
    > DISADVANTAGES:   You have already cut the fabric, so if it is too small,  your fabric is a loss.
    > SOLUTION:  Use in combination with  pattern measuring.

5.  A BETTER WAY?   You might try a combination of several of the above for best results at all times.
    > NOW:
    > > ...Get a good set of body measurements.
    > > ...Make a test pattern in 1/4" gingham checked fabric (NOT MUSLIN).  Let this gingham "fitting shell" help you discover how you differ from the commercial patterns.  (Use Vogue #2098.)  It takes about 3 yards of gingham.
    > > ...LEARN your MAJOR AND MINOR differences.

    > EACH TIME YOU SEW:
    > > ...Flat pattern measure (especially in problem areas areas).
    > > ...Alter pattern where necessary (for major problems).
    > > ...Fit as you sew. (This takes care of your minor problems.)

NOTE:  It is also helpful to find a friend who is willing to trade fitting help--preferably a neighbor or someone accessible.

## MAKING A GINGHAM FITTING SHELL

The checks really help point out fitting problems! The checks should go around the body at the bust and hip levels parallel to floor. The vertical checks should be perpendicular to the floor at the center front and center back. The side seams should hang straight down (approximately in the middle of the leg and not swing to the front or back).

This lady has a sloping shoulder and a high full hip. See what is happening to her checks.

Note: We designed Vogue #2098 Measure-Free ™ Body Fitting Guide ™ just for this technique. A PLUS - it also includes five pattern fronts - one for every bra cup size.

## THE NO-SLASH PATTERN ALTERATION METHOD

Pati has found this to be one of the easiest methods she has ever used to alter a pattern. It is also called the "pivot and slide method."

RULES:

Use the outline of your pattern as a cutting guide.

No need to cut into a pattern when using this method.

Cut around the pattern where you are making no changes, and then pivot or slide the pattern in order to make the necessary alterations.

Move the pattern back to original position to mark the darts. *MAY NEED TO MOVE DART*

## SLIDING THE PATTERN

### TO ADD WIDTH

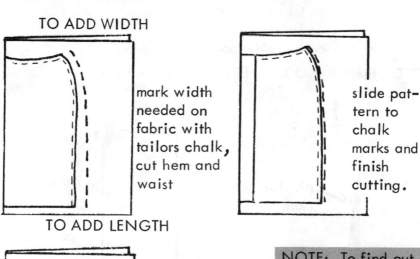

mark width needed on fabric with tailors chalk, cut hem and waist

slide pattern to chalk marks and finish cutting.

### TO ADD LENGTH

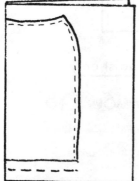

cut edges without change

slide to chalk marks and finish cutting

NOTE: To find out how much you need to add when cutting divide amount needed by 4 (the number of side seam allowances). Do not add to center front or back.

This method is used instead of sliding in places where you need to change one end of a line and not the other. For example, you need more at the waist in a bodice, but want the size of the armhole to remain the same.

## ON A BODICE

you have added to pattern in this manner

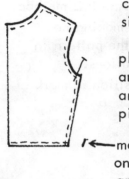

cut all but side seam

place pin at under-arm seam intersection and remove all other pins in pattern

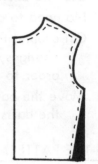

mark amount needed on fabric with chalk and pivot -- finish cutting side seam

NOTE: There is NO CHANGE at the pivot point.

## ON A SKIRT

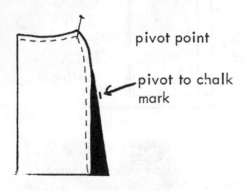

pivot point

pivot to chalk mark

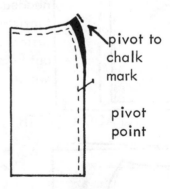

pivot to chalk mark

pivot point

To add to <u>hip only</u>

To add to <u>waist only</u>

NOTE: Be sure to pivot or slide the SAME AMOUNT TO FRONT AND BACK PIECES.

76

## FLAT DERRIERE

Skirt will sag in back. Side seams swing forward. Skirt is longer in back. There is too much length over and across fanny.

Correct by cutting excess off top at center back (may pivot down) and by cutting off side (may slide).

OR correct by taking a vertical tuck and one horizontal at center back to nothing at sides.

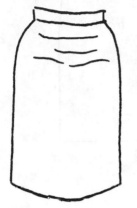
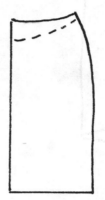
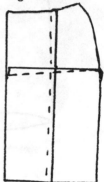

## HIGH HIP ON ONE SIDE

Skirt is shorter on high side.

Correct by raising pattern on sides. Cut off of side that is normal when fitting.

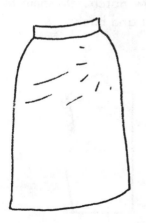

## FULL TUMMY

Wrinkles point to tummy.
Skirt is shorter in front.
Side seams swing forward.

Add to center front tapering to nothing at sides.
This gives "more length" to go OVER full tummy.

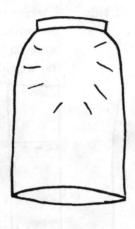

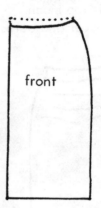

front

## SLOPING SHOULDERS

Wrinkles point down from neck.

Lower shoulder by pivoting down from neck. If armhole is too tight, lower below notch. Do same to front and back.

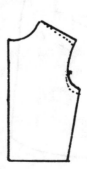

# SQUARE SHOULDERS

A sure sign of this is horizontal wrinkles across back of neck.

Raise shoulder by pivoting up from neck. Armhole may then be too large, so raise it same amount below notch. Do same on front and back.

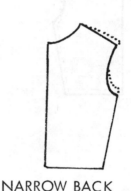

## WIDE BACK

Spread pattern in shoulder area.

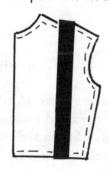

## NARROW BACK

Take a tuck in shoulder area parallel to grain.

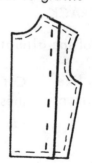

## ERECT OR SWAY BACK

Take a tuck at center back to nothing at sides. Try taking tucks in various places to see which does the best job. Try the pattern on after taking the tuck to see if it is short enough.

here
or
here →

to noth-ing

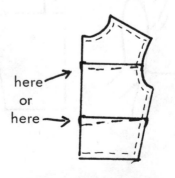

## WIDE SHOULDERS

Pivot the pattern out.

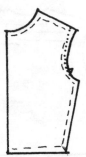

## NARROW SHOULDERS

Pivot the pattern in and cut narrower. We usually wait until the garment is together and simply trim off this excess in fitting.

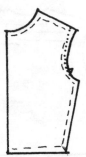

## ROUNDED BACK

This is one of the alterations that is easier to do by cutting into the pattern.

Often looks like this in a garment.

Cut pattern on these lines.

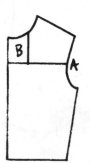

Spread across back (A) until neckline is raised enough to meet yours. Spread (B) until center back is straight. Make (B) into a neck dart 2-3" long so neck isn't enlarged.

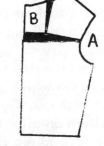

## THE BUSTLINE

This is another of the alterations that you really can't pivot or slide to achieve. It is easiest to cut into the pattern.

Patterns are made for the "average" size B bra cup. If you measure 40" around the bust but have 30" of it in front --- the "average" pattern will not fit you. If you have a size A or C bra cup, you may not have to worry on most patterns, especially the looser styles. If you are a D or DD --- chances are you'd better know how to make the alteration for full bust, or you will be buying patterns that are much too large in the shoulders in order to fit your bust.

WOULDN'T IT BE NICE---if pattern companies drew cutting lines on their patterns for the different bra cup sizes. It would look like this:

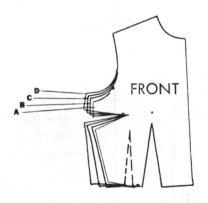

In an article in the Jan. 1972 issue of the Journal of Home Economics, Iowa State University instructor Norma Hollen suggests this idea to pattern com- panies. And, in 1979 Vogue became the first pattern company to include bra cup sizes in a pattern, Vogue #2098.

In the same article, Earline Strickland suggests the method on page 82 for altering the bust for a larger bra cup size. It's as easy as 1 - 2 - 3. This alteration will give you the extra length and width you need to go over your fuller bust.

81

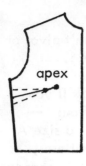
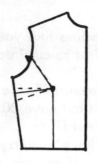

1. Draw a line through dart to point of bust (apex).

2. Draw a line from waist to Apex parallel to grain and then to notch.

3. Cut along lines to but not through points indicated by the dots.

Armhole size is not changed.

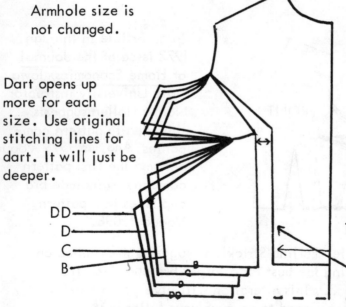

Dart opens up more for each size. Use original stitching lines for dart. It will just be deeper.

DD
D
C
B

At arrow, spread a minimum of:
1/2" for C cup
3/4" for D cup
1 1/4" for DD cup

you may want to add a dart here or take side seam in if too large.

As the bust dart opens wider, the bottom gets lower. Even it up across front.

# BUST DARTS

## WHERE IS MY "APEX"

1. Locate your apex (point of bust). Measure from center of your shoulder seam (1) to apex (2) and from apex to center front (3). Be sure your bra is adjusted correctly (if you wear one).

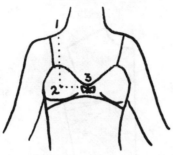

2. Darts should point to apex but end 1" away from point of bust ( unless style looks best with it closer ).

3. Find apex on pattern by measuring from shoulder seam (1) same distance down as to your apex (2) and from center front (3) toward apex. Mark your apex where the two-lines cross.

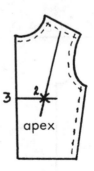

ALTERNATE METHOD: Pin pattern pieces together. Pin in darts. Try the tissue on. This will quickly give you an excellent idea of whether your darts are too high or too low.

## HOW TO MOVE A DART

To lower a dart either lower the point and redraw

or

Lower all three points same amount and redraw

For princess seaming, cut and spread above bust. Take out equal amounts below.

spread

tuck

## TO SHORTEN A DART

## TO LENGTHEN A DART

## HOW TO ADD A DART WHEN YOU NEED A DART

Find apex

Draw center line of dart (anywhere you want it) stop 1" from apex

Make dart as wide as you war and draw lines to point

84

## WITH NO DART

Many shirt patterns do not have darts. They do have extra
ease totally, but it may not be enough for a D bra cup size.
If the shirt is too tight across the front, add width and length
by using the alteration method on page 82. This will also
ADD that NEEDED DART, making the **shirt** fit better.

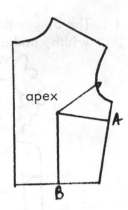

1. Find apex (easiest way is
   by trying pattern on).

2. Draw line (A) where
   you would like a dart.

3. Draw line (B) from apex
   to armscye notch and
   vertically below apex.

4. Spread amount needed.

5. Insert tissue.

6. Draw darts. (Make sure
   they point to the apex.)
   The beginning of the dart
   should be as wide as the
   opening (even if you move
   it over as we did the vertical
   dart in the illustration).

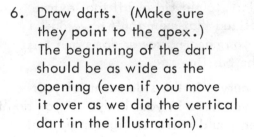

## FIT AS YOU SEW

This is the key to perfection! Try your garment on during each step of construction before a full length mirror. See how it looks and hangs. (SMILE---it'll look better if you smile, even if only partially made!)

KEEP IN MIND THESE TWO POINTS BEFORE BEGINNING:

1. The bigger the BODY BUMPS, the more length, width, and deeper darts they will need.

NOTE: Pati used to think that people with small busts needed to take deeper darts to get rid of all that extra fullness. She finally realized that men don't have darts! If you are flat chested, you need narrower darts and less length and width over the bustline.

2. Sew the same curves in the side seams of your garment that you have in your body. If you don't have any, then you'd better straighten up that side seam.

## PREPARE GARMENT

1. Cut pattern making necessary adjustments
2. Mark darts
3. Staystitch (Important since you will be fitting)
4. Sew darts and all seams but side seams
5. Pin baste side seams
6. Try on for fit
7. Sew side seams (deeper if too big, narrower if tight)

1. Cut pattern to fit. See pivot and slide section.

2. Mark all three lines of dart and a line at the end to show you where to stop stitching.

3. Staystitch directionally.

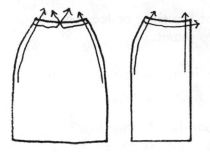

4. Sew darts.

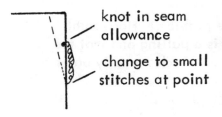

knot in seam allowance

change to small stitches at point

5. Sew zipper in back or front.

6. With right sides together, **pin baste** side seams for fitting. (This is much faster than machine or hand basting but also MORE DANGEROUS! OUCH!! Therefore, point pins downward.) Turn right side out and try on.

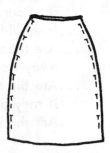

7. If it fits, sew side seams permanently. If not, **pin** tighter or looser and try on again.

8. Tie 1/4" elastic around top of skirt with bottom of elastic at 5/8" seam line (waistline). Check the HANG of the skirt. Adjust skirt under elastic until grain at hip level is parallel to floor and side seams are perpendicular to floor.

1. Fit from the top down. CHECK POINTS:
   - ...Are the shoulder seams in the center of the shoulder ?
   - ...Is shoulder width correct ?
   - ...Are the darts pointing to the bust, yet 1/2" away from point of bust or "apex"?
   - ...Are the skirt darts too long.? They will pucker if they go past the fullest part of your body.
   - ...Are the side seams hanging straight?

2. Check the ease. Is the garment too tight or too loose? If so, take in or let out the side seams.

3. Are the side seams running vertical and perpendicular to floor?

4. Is the crosswise grain running parallel to the floor? Unfortunately, it is not always possible to see the the grainline in a fabric. If you can't, use number 5 as a suggestion.

5. Wrinkles usually point to the problem! Horizontal wrinkles usually mean there is a pulling and that the garment is too tight. Slanted wrinkles usually point to specific problems as below:

high full
hip on
one side

full
tummy

# YOU'LL NEVER AGAIN NEED TO MARK A HEM ON A SKIRT

<u>Where</u> do you even up an uneven hem???

AT THE TOP!! (The only exception is a bias garment.)

If a skirt is not hanging right, chances are that it is because of a full tummy, flat seat, or one hip higher than the other. You need to add more or less length to go over the problem.

HOW TO CHANGE THE TOP OF A SKIRT TO MAKE IT HANG EVENLY. Adjust elastic until skirt hangs evenly. Mark bottom with pins. Sew waistband on at new markings.

| Full tummy | High hip on one side | Flat seat |
|---|---|---|
| Front | Front and Back | Back |
| Raise band over tummy. | Raise band over high hip. | Lower band at center back. |

NOTE: Ideally, it is best to make the alterations in your pattern before you cut your fabric. See alteration section for more information. Of course, fitting as you sew may still be necessary as your pattern alterations may not have been completely accurate.

Mother Pletsch's Truths

PODIUM

There are some things in sewing that are just plain "truths"--
like the sun rises in the east and sets in the west. We can argue
and fiddle with new and different ways of sewing, but a few
truths remain.

## TRUTH #1

We wouldn't even mention "staystitching" in a painless
sewing book, but it's becoming more important to staystitch
now that woven fabrics are re-entering the fashion picture.
Use regular stitch length ( 10 - 12 stitches per inch ) and sew
1/2" from the edge. TO SAVE THREAD AND TIME, use the
CONTINUOUS method. Just feed one piece after another into
the machine and step on the accelerator and GO!

## TRUTH # 2

It is important to staystitch curved edges because they could stretch out. If you "fit as you sew," you should staystitch any raw edges that may get pulled on during the process whether they are straight grain or curves. You have probably heard the term DIRECTIONAL STAYSTITCHING. This means to staystitch in the "direction" of the grain. If you staystitch against the grain, you may stretch the edge just by stitching on it. How do you know which direction the grain is going? There are 3 ways to tell:

1. Staystitch from wide to narrow (i.e. from bottom to top on an A-line skirt.)

2. The direction the threads point.

yes        no

3. It's like stroking a kitty. Staystitch "with the fur", not against it

As a general rule, use these directions for a bodice and a skirt.

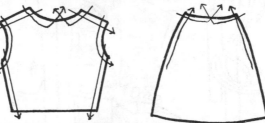

NOTE: When staystitching neck, pivot and sew off fabric edge. It makes snipping off those threads easier and also allows you to use the "continuous stitching" technique.

Fabrics that most need staystitching: loosely woven fabrics, ravelly fabrics, fabrics made from natural fibers, and inter-lock knits (on the edge that runs). We do not recommend staystitching synthetic single knits - the edges draw up and it is really unnecessary anyway.

## TRUTH # 3

Sometimes the things that seem like extra work are really time savers in the end --- like pressing a tissue pattern before cutting, like our friend Emilie does! It makes cutting faster and more accurate.

## TRUTH # 4

Do what you hate the most or think will be the hardest FIRST. Then the rest is psychologically super easy!

## TRUTH # 5

If you are unsure about how 2 pieces of unusual shape are sewn together, get out your pattern. Match the notches and dots.

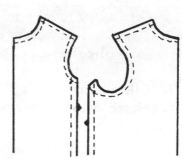

## TRUTH # 6

There are ways to make cutting easier:

1. If any seam is on the exact straight of grain, it may be eliminated by placing the seam line on the fold.
2. Many jacket and shirt fronts are made with a sew-on facing. Check to see if the grain is straight and eliminate the seam and make it a "cut-on" facing.
3. Cut straight seams on the selvage to eliminate seam finishing in woven fabrics. New fabrics don't draw up or shrink on the selvage like old ones did.
4. Change a 2 piece cuff to one.
5. How to avoid cutting frustration --- BUY ENOUGH FABRIC.

## TRUTH #7

Reducing bulk is one of the most important of our truths. A bulky enclosed seam can make a garment look very tacky. Before turning a collar, a pocket, or a faced neckline to the inside, try one of these ways of reducing bulk:

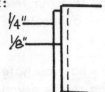

1. Trim seams to 1/4"
2. Grade or "layer" seam to 1/8"

NOTE: A speedy way to trim and grade in one step is to "bevel." Slant your scissors until they are almost flat over the seam and trim. This automatically makes the top layer shorter.

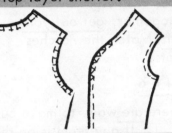

3. Clip inward curves
4. Notch outward curves

NOTE: For easy notching, use pinking shears. It's quick and smooth.

NOTE: Be sure to use small stitches whenever trimming, grading, notching, or clipping close to a seam line to prevent raveling.

## TRUTH #9

To further flatten an enclosed seam, use the understitching technique, which means to stitch the seam allowances to the facing. It is used mainly on necklines, collars and armholes. Use a regular stitch length and stitch 1/8" from well of seam. Use one of the following stitch types:

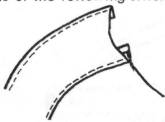

1. Straight stitch.

2. Blind hemming stitch.

*Pretty Pati's Pointers*

Pati always remembers things best when she knows the logic behind the concept ----so she teaches sewing in that way. Pati's pointers are basic ideas in sewing that apply to most sewing tasks, and they are ideas that make sewing so-o-o-o-o much easier. Many sewing books touch on these thoughts, but we want to emphatically emphasize them!

## POINTER # 1

How do you sew 2 edges together that are completely different in shape?

Straight collar

Curved neckline

1. Staystitch 1/2" from edge.

2. Clip to staystitching.

3. Spread neckline.

4. Pin collar in place.

5. Sew to neck edge.

How to "key" a facing to a neck, armhole, or top of skirt or pants to make it lie flat. (The ugliest thing is a facing that doesn't fit and shows on the outside.)

1. Lay front facing in place. Smooth flat and pin.
2. Where facing overlaps seam line, snip.

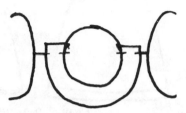

3. Fold front away from shoulder. Pin the back facing in place and snip where back falls over seam.

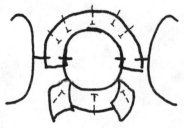

4. With facing ends right sides together, line up **snips** and stitch.

5. Trim facing seam to 1/4" and press open.

6. Match seam lines of facing and garment with pins through both seam lines.

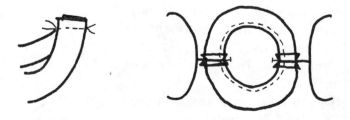

7. Stitch, trim, grade, understitch, and press.

97

# POINTER # 3

Our new phrase is "if the hem shows, it <u>must</u> be ready-made." With labor costs so high, ready-to-wear quality must suffer. It has even become a status thing to sew because of better quality and hems are the first indicator of quality.

How wide should a hem be?

Straight skirt 3"     A-line skirt 1 1/2" - 2 1/2"   Full circle 1/4" roll

NOTE: It is almost impossible to make an invisible hem in some soft light weight knits, especially jerseys and tricots. Designers have decided not to fight it and are reverting to a narrow 1/4" hem, even on slimmer skirts. They either turn the hem up once or twice and topstitch (one turn is best, it is less bulky), or they turn it up twice and hand slip stitch. The alternative would be a 1 - 1 1/2" hem with <u>very</u> loose hand stitches. The narrower the better! Do not use seam bindings, hem laces, or zig-zag finishes. They are too bulky and often leave an ugly impression on these light weight knits.

## Hemming steps:

1. Turn up desired hem and press crease "lightly." NEVER press over top edge of a hem. It may leave a permanent impression on the right side.
2. Grade seams in hem allowance to 1/4".
3. If necessary, ease hem edge to fit skirt. Try stretch lace seam tape---a 40¢ sanity saver.

## How to use stretch lace.

...Fold up hem, match seam allowances
and pin together.
...Use the same amount of lace
as distance from seam to seam
of garment. Pin lace on from
seam to seam.
...Sew lace to hem edge with
lace side on top. The feed
dogs of the machine will ease
the excess hem edge into the
lace. If they don't, gently
stretch lace until it "uses up"
the excess hem.

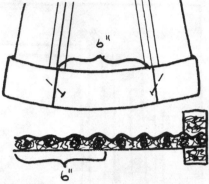

NOTE: We like Talon lace seam tape because it has a
pretty scalloped edge that curves well with hem edges.

## Another way to ease a hem.

...Stitch with a long basting stitch 1/4" from the edge of hem.
...Pull up on bobbin thread until hem is eased enough to fit
garment.

## Hemming with the "designer hem stitch."

This technique is recommended for invisible hems, not
necessarily durable hems! Do not use in children's things
and re-learn how to carefully step into your own clothes.
...Turn the hem edge back.
...Use polyester thread. It wears longer and you'll never have
a hem come out because the thread broke.
...Take long loose stitches catching only a single fiber of your
outside fabric. (Use the smallest needle you can thread---
a size 10 sharp is best.)
...Every few stitches, pull to loosen them and secure by knotting
in hem allowance. This will protect you in case you accidentally step into your hem.

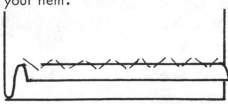

# Hemming with fusible webs.

1.  Crease hem edge with iron.
2.  Grade seam in hem to 1/4".
3.  Cut strip of fusible web 1/4" narrower than hem width.
4.  Place web to fold line.

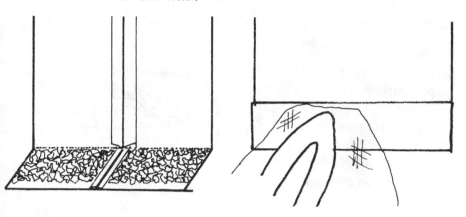

5.  Turn up hem and steam press for 2 seconds in each spot (steam basting temporarily holds hem in place). Be sure to use a see-through press cloth.

NOTE: If you accidentally get fusible web on your iron, use one of the hot-iron cleaners available in your notions department.

6. If hem looks smooth, you are ready to fuse. Steam for 10 - 15 seconds in each spot. Do not press over top edge or you will create an imprint on the right side.

NOTE: We recommend this method primarily for polyester double knit fabric. It is great for hemming men's knit pants. AND FAST TOO!! Always test a piece of fusible web with a scrap of your fabric to make sure you like the look and feel.

Stitching in the ditch (the well of the seam) is not a new technique by any means, but a very helpful one that has a 100 uses.   One of our favorite uses is for a band.

... Topstitch from outside in the well of the seam. This catches the band on the underside .

This edge must be finished unless it is a knit. For woven fabrics it must be on the selvage or zig-zagged to prevent raveling.

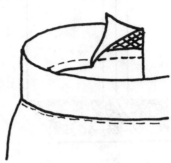

Other uses.

| Quickie cuff | Stand up collars | Tacking facings down |
|---|---|---|

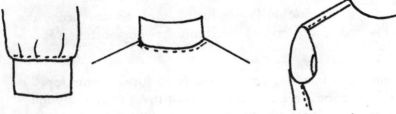

Quickie self-binding on knit tops

In seams to keep elastic from rolling

An inside curve, like an inner cylinder, must be smaller. Wherever 2 layers of fabric go around your body together, you should make the inside layer smaller. This allows for what is termed "turn of cloth."

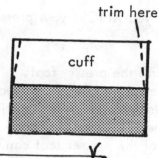

At the end of a waistband or cuff, trim 1/8" off the under side to nothing at fold line.

Make sure the edges meet when you sew the ends together.

There is "turn of cloth" in a collar, also. The upper collar rolls over the under collar creating an inner cylinder.

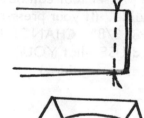

Trim 1/8" off (1/4" for very heavy fabrics) from center front to center front. If collar points are very acutely angled, trim little or nothing off at points or you won't be able to sew them together.

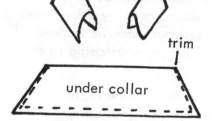

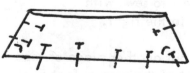

Match edges of upper and under collar when you sew them together. This creates a "bubble" in upper collar which will disappear when collar is completed.

Other places "turn of cloth" is evident.

...Trim lining smaller in "lined-to-edge" vest so it won't
   show. See page 56.

...Make underlining smaller so that it won't sag inside.
   See page 51 for glue and fold technique.

## POINTER # 6

   If you KNOW your presser foot, topstitching will be
easy !

Measure the presser foot.
Most measure 1/4" from needle
to outside edge. Most topstitching
is done 1/4" from the edge, so the
edge of the presser foot can be
used as a guide. (If your presser
foot measures 3/8", CHANGE the
standard and USE what YOUR presser
foot measures as a guide.)

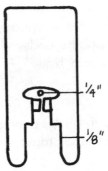

Help yourself sew accurate width
seam allowances by using masking
tape on your machine marked off
for easy-to-see stitching lines.

Be sure to put tape on left
side of presser foot also,
since there are times when
it is best to sew with
fabric to the right.

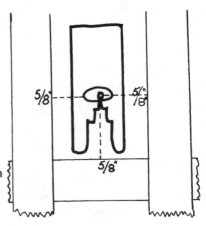

Also, put another piece of tape
in front of the presser foot 5/8"
from the needle to help you when
pivoting around a corner.

# Press As You Sew

There are many places to cut corners and cheat in sewing, but eliminating pressing as you sew is not one of them. We firmly believe that even a so-called "sewing disaster" can be made wearable by good pressing techniques. A good pressing can hide a multitude of sins!

Pressing is another one of the places where the right tools for the task are a necessity. Susan sews a great deal during her travels and yet wherever she travels her suitcase of pressing aids follows. She swears she can't sew without them!

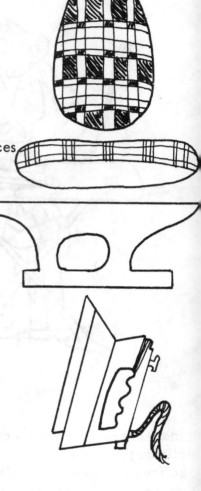

1. Pressing ham (tailor's ham) –
   a ham-shaped surface ideal for
   pressing curved and shaped areas,
   helps give "people shape" to
   flat fabric.
2. Seam roll – a sausage-shaped
   gadget used to press open flat
   seams and cylinders like sleeves
   and pant legs. The seam allowances
   fall over the edge of the roll and
   allow your iron to touch only the
   stitching line itself.
3. Point presser/clapper – a wooden
   combination tool used to press
   open seams and points, and to
   flatten a seam by holding steam
   in fabric.
4. See-through press cloths – sheer
   cloth you can see through so you
   can see what you're doing!
5. "Shot of Steam" type-iron – a
   super steaming iron with an
   extra button to press for a jet of
   steam that will press even the
   most stubborn fabric.

You can purchase the above five pressing aids for a total in-
vestment of about $40 and half of that is for the iron. If you see
other nifty items (and there are literally 100's of additional
pressing aids on the market today), put them on your "buy this for
me sometime" list.

## BROWN PAPER BAG MYSTIQUE

Why does every sewing reference book written tell us to press using "Brown Paper"? What magical, mystical powers does Brown Paper have that blue paper or white paper lack? NONE, WE INSIST! The objective is to place a piece of heavy paper under each seam allowance to prevent a ridge or indentation from showing on the right side of the seam. So why can't it be the envelope from your telephone bill, a piece of notebook paper (folded in half if one layer is too lightweight to do the job) or last month's birthday card? We think cutting strips of "Brown Paper" sounds like a pain! Besides, you can avoid almost the entire issue by using the seam roll you just bought!

## HOW TO PRESS

### A SEAM

1. Press flat first to remove any puckers.

2. Place over seam roll. Saturate with steam by holding iron 1/8" above fabric surface.

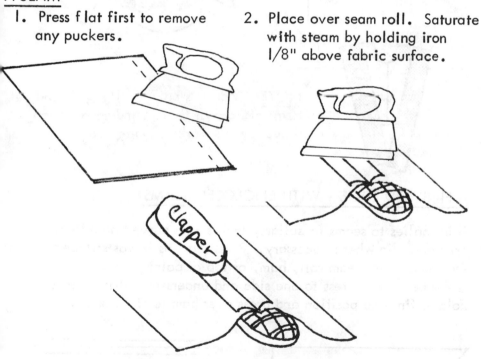

3. Place point presser/clapper on top of seam and apply light pressure. The clapper used to be called a pounding block because fabrics were actually pounded into shape, but today's fabrics just need gentle pressure, not a beating.

## A DART

Press dart as it was stitched to flatten fold line and to blend stitches together. Place the dart over the appropriate curve of the ham and tuck paper under fold to prevent an indentation from showing on the right side.

NOTE: The ham is filled with moldable sawdust and can be pounded to make any shape of curve needed for darts. Bust darts go over a very round curve and skirt darts over a flatter one.

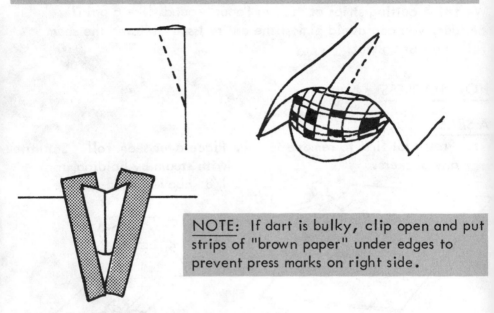

NOTE: If dart is bulky, clip open and put strips of "brown paper" under edges to prevent press marks on right side.

## A FINISHED EDGE – WITH ENCLOSED SEAMS

This applies to seams in collars, lapels and curved necklines. Trim and clip where necessary. Press seam as it was stitched. Press seam open over seam roll, ham, or top of point presser (whichever is the best fit). Press to one side and understitch if necessary. Fold to finished position and press over ham to final press.

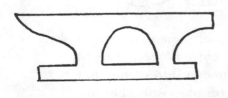

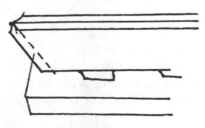

## A SET - IN SLEEVE

Always press the seam allowance from the inside of the sleeve. DO NOT press the seam open nor top-press the sleeve cap.

## PRESSING TIPS

1. Press with an "up and down" motion of the iron whenever possible, otherwise slide iron along seam in ONE direction in order to make a smooth seam.

2. Vertical darts are pressed toward the center for consistency.

3. Horizontal darts are pressed up. We're not just trying to be different, we think this gives a smoother, higher-busted, younger look.

4. Fingers are a FREE pressing tool! You can slightly finger press a seam or dart in the right direction BEFORE permanently pressing with the iron or pounding block.

5. Pressing takes PATIENCE!! Too speedy pressing can create an overpressed, shiny, "I'm old and worn" look in a new fabric. Synthetic fabrics will overpress more quickly than natural fabrics because the fibers are more heat sensitive, so use a very light touch with these.

6. Top-pressing in our book is a YES YES, not no no! Most pressing should be done from the inside to prevent the possible shine or over-press, but do press when construction pressing hasn't quite done the trick. Use a press cloth always, fingerpress if possible, and use gentle pressure on the iron or clapper.

7. Press lightly - If it isn't flat enough at first then lightly press again. And again. And again. Much better than too much the first time for a shiny, old look.

109

# Necessary Details

"Having trouble with sleeves and cuffs?"

## SET-IN SLEEVES

The term "set-in sleeve" often brings tears to the eyes of even the heartiest home sewer - yet it doesn't have to. Thank goodness patterns have changed throughout the years so sleeves are really much easier to do today. But there are still many tricks that can make any sleeve a snap to sew. We feel sleeves are even EASIER than sleeveless faced armholes!

The following work order for making a sleeve seems to be the easiest in achieving a professional looking sleeve:

> 1. Complete the placket.*
> 2. Complete the cuffs.
> 3. Sew cuff to sleeve.
> 4. Set the sleeve into armscye.

*EXCEPTION: Complete placket after #3 if using "Marta's Special" method on page 115.

We will give you several methods for completing each step. Why not try them all and find the one you like best. We'd like to point out that some of the "easy-quickie" methods are not always the best. For example, the easiest placket doesn't look good if you like to turn your cuffs back.

We will attack one part of the sleeve at a time in the order they are "usually" completed: placket, cuff, and sleeve.

READ ON.....

With the exception of Pati -- concensus of opinion ruled that the traditional continuous placket is a PAIN! How then do we get a finished slit to allow a cuff to button? READ ON --

## FACED PLACKET

1. Cut sleeve.

2. Snip mark location of placket.

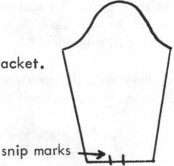

snip marks

3. Cut two 2" X 3" bias rectangles of matching fabric. (You may use your fashion fabric, matching lining, or fusible interfacing.)

NOTE: Try Armo's new Fuseaknit or Stacy's new Easy-Knit -- they don't come in a full color range, but the few basic colors are likely to blend with your fabric. They are also ravel resistant-- a big help!

4. Pin to right side of sleeve with right sides together. Center over snips.

5. Stitch a "V" 2 inches long.  Be sure to use very tiny stitches near the point and when you pivot at the point to come down the other side of "V", leave your needle in the fabric.

6. Slash to point, turn, and press.  It won't ravel if you used small stitches at point.

7. Cut patch of fusible web 1 1/2" X 2 1/2", slash the web the length of the placket opening.  Place web between facing and sleeve.  Fuse in place.

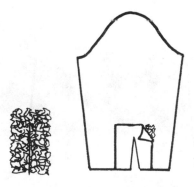

NOTE: If using a fusible knit, just press and it will fuse in place.

(This is not really a placket in the true sense, as there is no actual opening.)

1. Cut sleeve.
2. Snip mark in the center of pattern placket marking.

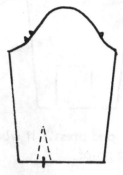

3. To reinforce opening, stitch on 5/8" seam line for 1" on both sides of snip.

4. Clip to seam line 1/2" on both sides of snip mark.

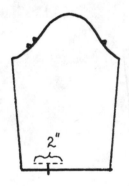

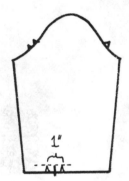

5. Fold 1" section twice to inside and topstitch or slipstitch in place.

## MARTA'S PAINLESS PLACKET...THE "WHEN ALL ELSE FAILS, TURN THE PLACKET INTO A SEAM" PLACKET

This method was found to be a lifesaver when we all started working on Ultrasuede several years ago. Marta found a pattern already designed this way and has since used it as her "only" sleeve for shirts and shirt jackets. Since not every pattern has such a sleeve, Marta began showing her students how to convert a regular sleeve from an underarm seam to a side back seam.

CAUTION: This technique is best for a straight sleeve. Because they are awkward to work with we don't advise it for a full, fitted, or sleeve with a flat cap.

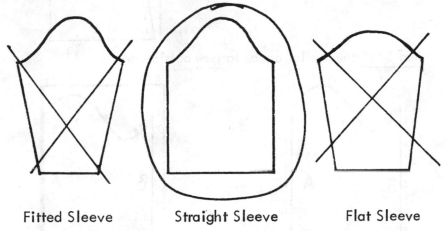

Fitted Sleeve          Straight Sleeve          Flat Sleeve

1. Draw a line through the center of the pattern placket markings parallel to the grain.

2. Cut along that line.

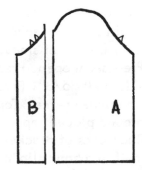

3. Reposition B so that the existing stitching lines overlap.

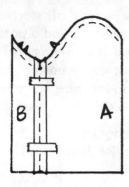

4. If the sleeve is not completely straight, over-lap underarm dots (X) and line up cut edges until parallel. Tape together.

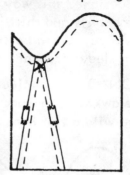

5. Add 5/8" seam allowances to new outside edges.

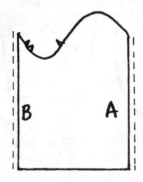

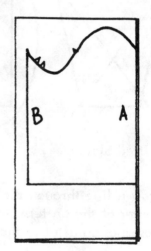

6. Cut edge A on selvage.

7. Attach cuff.
8. Begin sewing sleeve seam 3" from bottom of sleeve.
9. Press seam open. Press selvage side under 5/8". Press other side under twice. Topstitch around placket opening.
10. Tuck ends of placket into cuff and hand slip stitch under cuff to sleeve.

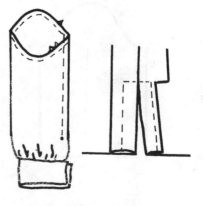

It can be sewed on completely flat <u>before</u> the sleeve seam is sewn.

1. Measure cuff pattern around your wrist to make sure cuff fits properly. It should overlap at least 1/2" and not more than an inch. If in doubt, make sure pattern's button and buttonhole markings overlap.

2. Apply cuff before sewing sleeve into garment.

3. You may stitch ends of cuff either before or after stitching it to sleeve.

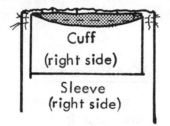

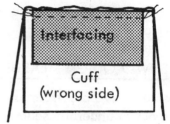

4. You may wish to allow an extension on the under cuff side     OR     you may sew ends even with placket edge

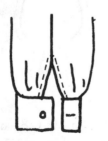

If in doubt, pin cuff to sleeve and try sleeve on your arm and overlap where it would be buttoned. See how it looks. Just make sure placket either overlaps or at least comes together so your skin doesn't show.

## SLEEVES

### BEFORE YOU CUT, CHECK THE EASE

A quick check on size of a sleeve cap will help you get a pucker-free sleeve. Note the following:

1. Traditional ease in a sleeve cap is 1 1/2". This works best in loosely woven fabrics made from natural fibers, such as wool. Natural fibers absorb steam and you can shrink in fullness with an iron.
2. It is best to reduce the ease to 1" in synthetic or permanent press fabrics that are very tightly woven.
3. We also reduce the ease in the sleeve cap for most knits, because knits give and don't need all that extra fullness. It is difficult to ease more then 1" into some knits, such as nylon tricots.

### TAKE TWO QUICK MEASUREMENTS TO CHECK EASE

Measure sleeve cap from under-arm seam to underarm seam.

Measure armscyes from under-arm seam to underarm seam.

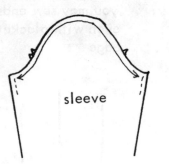

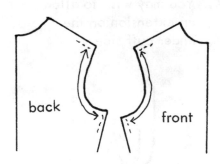

To reduce cap to 1" - begin at notch and trim off 1/8" at top of cap. "Impossible to ease" fabrics may need more trimming.

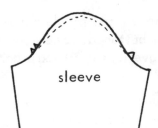

trim 1/8" off top to nothing at notches

## SETTING IN A SLEEVE

1. Easing the cap:

### SUSAN'S METHOD

Machine baste 2 rows of stitching from notch to notch over the sleeve cap. Place one row at 1/2" and the other at 3/4" from the edge. Stitch between the two rows when setting in a sleeve.

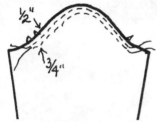

pull up on both threads

### PATI'S METHOD

Machine baste 2 rows of stitching from notch to notch. Place one row at 3/8" and the other at 5/8" from the edge. Pull up on the 3/8" stitching line only. The 5/8" line is only a guide for your final stitching.

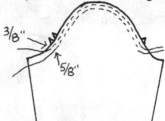

pull up on 3/8" thread only

NOTE: Place as little as possible ease in the top 2" of sleeve as it is on the straight of grain. This prevents puckering and pleating at the top.

2. If you have a long sleeve with a cuff, finish the bottom.

3. Place sleeve in armscye matching underarm seams and pin. The second pin goes into the top of the sleeve, and the next two pins join the notches. Add any extra pins you need to make the ease even.

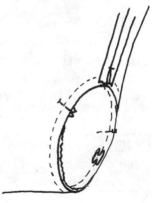

4. Machine baste sleeve in place and check for puckers on right side. Smooth seam with your thumb and forefinger. Clip and re-stitch if there are puckers.

119

## 5. Final stitching:

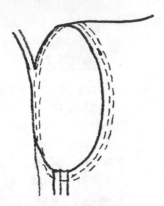

...Restitch sleeve on 5/8" line.
Stitch another row 1/4" from
seam line.

...Trim to 1/4" around armscye.

NOTE: The second row of stitching may be a zig-zag.

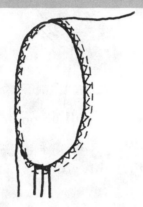

NOTE: No more popped sleeve seams. A stretch-overlock
stitch is Pati's favorite. It is the one-step finish accomplish-
ing the first and second row at the same time. Trim to 1/4"
after stitching. If you use the stretch-overlock stitch, your
sleeve will NEVER rip out.

NOTE: For additional really nifty new ideas in setting in sleeves,
see our books Sewing Skinner® Ultrasuede® Fabric and Easy, Easier
Easiest Tailoring.

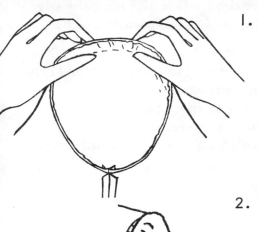

1. Rub and pull on seam with thumbs and fore-fingers. The machine basting is loose enough to allow some smoothing.

2. Clip the basting from the outside and pull seam apart. Smooth more full-ness into other areas of the sleeve including the cap or the underarm area if necessary.

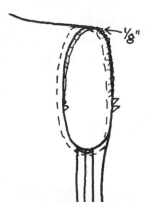

3. Slip sleeve cap 1/8" in cap area.

4. When all else fails, place as much fullness at the very top 2" and call it a gathered sleeve!

# OTHER SET-IN-SLEEVE METHODS

## SHIRT-TYPE SLEEVE----THE FLAT METHOD

For most people, the flat method is the easiest, but it is not always the prettiest. It is usually used only for men's shirts when a flat-felled underarm seam is desired. It is also the only way you can set a sleeve into the tiny armhole of a small child's garment.

1. Stitch shoulder seam of garment. Leave garment and side seam and sleeve underarm seam open.
2. Machine baste two rows of ease stitching around cap.
3. Make placket if you have a long sleeve.
4. Pin sleeve into armhole matching notches. Adjust ease. Stitch.

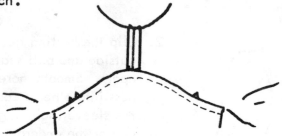

5. Pin underarm seam of garment and sleeve. Stitch a continuous seam from bottom of garment to bottom of sleeve. Press open.

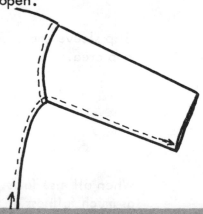

You might finish with a mock flat-fell finish. Topstitch both seam allowances to one side.

NOTE: There are two disadvantages of this method. It does not work with "Marta's Painless Placket" method and the underarm seam intersection is very bulky. Therefore, we discourage it on anything but a man's shirt or a child's garment.

## MODIFIED FLAT METHOD

This method incorporates the speed of the flat method and the superior fit of the conventionally set-in sleeve.

1. After easing sleeve cap, pin to armhole matching notches. Adjust ease. Stitch from notch to notch only.

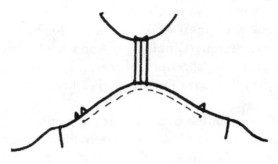

2. Stitch garment and sleeve underarm seam. Press open.

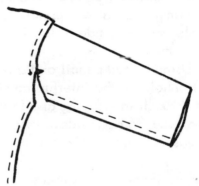

3. Match sleeve and garment underarm seams and complete stitching armscye seam from notch to notch underarm.

4. Finish seam and trim to 1/4".

123

# BUTTONHOLES

## HAND WORKED (painful)  MACHINE (easy)  BOUND (beautiful)

  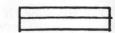

## WHERE TO USE THE DIFFERENT TYPES?

1. Blouses---generally use machine .
2. Blazers---look the nicest when bound buttonholes are used, however, some designers,including Anne Klein, use machine buttonholes on their "sportier" blazers. They have machines that do "keyhole" shapes that look like hand worked button-holes.
3. Shirt jackets---machine because they are sporty.
4. Coats---bound are the nicest and wear the longest, however in a sporty coat, machine buttonholes are acceptable.

## HINTS FOR MARKING BUTTONHOLE PLACEMENT

Machine---Simply use a lead pencil and lightly dot each end of buttonhole on right side of fabric. They will disappear when you sew over them.

Bound --- Using a lead pencil and a ruler, mark the center and ends of buttonhole on the interfacing side. Machine baste on these lines through interfacing and fashion fabric in order to transfer markings to right side. (Use a contrast color bobbin thread for easy-to-see markings.)

NOTE: All horizontal buttonholes begin 1/8" toward edge from center front.

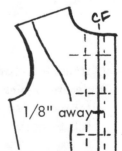

NOTE: For speed, Pati makes all bound buttonholes 1" long and 1/4" wide. She hates to select her buttons ahead of time. This way she can buy 3/4 - 1" buttons later--they all seem to look fine.

## HINTS FOR MACHINE BUTTONHOLES

1. If they are not full enough, sew around twice.
2. Clip open by folding in half and clipping with embroidery scissors.

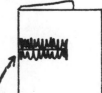

# HINTS FOR OUR FAVORITE BOUND BUTTONHOLE

1. Pin bias strips of matching lining (such as Poly-SiBonne) 1" longer than buttonhole and 1-1/2" wide on right side of garment centered over placement lines. Do not use all polyester or permanent press fabrics. They won't press flat.

2. Machine baste through center of lining. (Easiest when done from wrong side--you can follow basting lines more easily.)

3. Using small stitches, stitch a rectangle the length of the buttonhole and 1/4" wide (1/8" on either side of the center line). Use the edge of your metal presser foot as a stitching guide. Start and stop stitching at "X" to avoid weak corners.

4. Clip rectangle. If you used very small stitches, you will not weaken buttonhole by clipping all the way to corners.

NOTE: Clip from center to corner in order to form larger wedges at each end.

5. Turn lining to wrong side. A "window" is formed.

NOTE: For SPEED--pin lining down into pressing ham to get a good press.

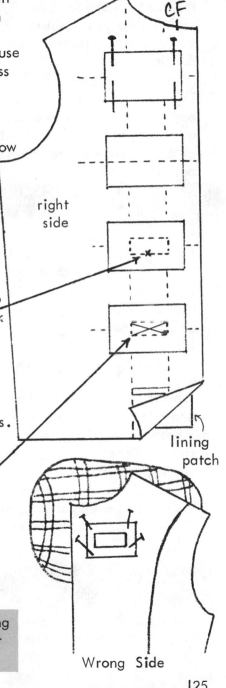

right side

CF

lining patch

Wrong Side

6. Prepare lips by basting 2 pieces of fashion fabric right sides together through the center. Use straight grain unless your fashion fabric is plaid and you want the lips on the bias.

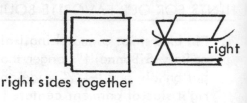

right

right sides together

7. A speedy method for centering lips without pinning or basting———cut a piece of fusible web with a rectangle cut out of the center the size of your buttonhole "window."

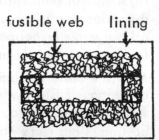

fusible web    lining

NOTE: To cut a window in the web, fold the rectangle in half and clip out a piece half the length of the buttonhole and 1/4" wide.

Place the web on the wrong side of buttonhole over the lining patch. "Steam baste" web in place by lightly steaming web until it becomes tacky and adheres to lining patch———do not touch iron to web.

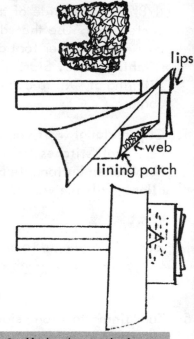

lips

web

lining patch

8. From right side, center lips under "window" and fuse using a press cloth. Lips will now stay in place without slipping while you stitch.

9. Fold back fashion fabric exposing ends. Using a zipper foot, stitch lining to lips. Do both ends, then sides.

NOTE: For SPEED, do the same end of all the buttonholes at one time continuously.

10. Trim and grade back side of buttonhole. Hand catch stitch to interfacing.

126

1. Pin facing in place smoothly over the back of buttonholes.

2. Put bias strips of lining on right side of facing over buttonhole area. (Do this by "feel" from right side of garment and use 2" X 3" pieces of lining to make sure they cover buttonhole area.)

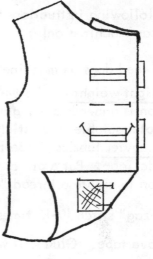

3. Stick pins straight down through ends of buttonholes .

4. Draw a pencil line on lining patch from pin to pin. This marks the center of the buttonhole.

5. Place two additional pins across ends of buttonholes and take first pins out.

6. Machine baste over center line from pin to pin.

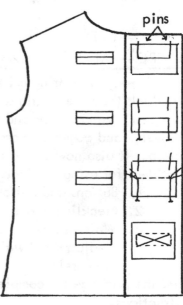

pins

7. Stitch a rectangle and clip to corners as in #3 page 125.

8. Turn lining patch to wrong side and press.

9. Steam baste a rectangle of fusible web to lining patch.

10. Fuse "window" in facing to back of buttonhole.

## SEW YOUR BUTTONS ON BY MACHINE!  WE DO!

Use the following instructions for "sew-through" buttons and on zig-zag machines only:

1.  Drop feed dogs on machine or turn to "0" stitch length.
2.  For light weight fabrics where a "shank" underneath the button is unnecessary , glue button in place with a dot of water soluble  glue stick.
    For heavier fabrics , tape the button in place with Scotch Magic Tape.  Put a pin or wooden matchstick underneath button to create a thread "shank."
3.  Zig-zag" stitch 10-15 times.
4.  Remove tape.  Glue will wash out.


## VELCRO®---AN EASY CLOSURE

OK -- you've tried all the buttonhole methods and you still think they are a pain -- then VELCRO is your answer. The "new" Velcro hook and loop fastener is lighter in weight, stronger,  and comes in more sizes and shapes than the old Velcro. It also now comes in colors and is "self-basting." It is ideal for using in place of the following:
1.  Buttons and buttonholes
2.  Neckline hooks and snaps
3.  Waistline hooks or buttons. (Just think--an "adjustable" waistband for those great holiday dinners!)
Read the package for complete where-to-use and how-to instructions.

NOTE:  Velcro - like every other closure - should be CLOSED before laundering.

## ZIPPERS

The easiest zipper to use is the invisible zipper; the easiest time to sew in a zipper is while the fabrics are still flat; and the easiest place to put any zipper is in the center front, center back, or side back (they are straighter seam allowances and fitting can be done from the side seams without the need to redo the zipper). But the VERY EASIEST thing we can say about zippers isn't about the zipper at all---it is about Talon® Basting Tape. This double-faced skinny tape has made the no-pin, no-baste zipper an easy reality. Buy two rolls. You'll love it!.

### INVISIBLE ZIPPER

### CONVENTIONAL ZIPPER

Use Talon Basting Tape for preventing slippage and puckering, matching plaids, stripes, and prints, matching waistline seams and yokes where they cross the zipper.

Use Talon Basting Tape to prevent creeping and slipping while machine stitching and eliminate the need for pinning or basting during application.

Stick Talon Basting Tape along both the left and right sides of the face of the zipper, as close to the edge of the tape as possible.

NOTE: Try Talon Basting Tape for holding together fabrics that may slip during stitching such as Ultrasuede, leather and synthetic leathers, and plaids.

# AN EASY CONVENTIONAL ZIPPER METHOD

1. Sew seam up to zipper opening and knot.

2. Make underlap by pressing under 1/2" on right side of skirt back.

   Make overlap by pressing under under 5/8" on left side of skirt back .

3. Stick Talon Basting Tape (T.B.T.) to both sides of face of zipper on very edge. Peel away protective paper on right side only.

4. Stick zipper to underlap side and stitch in place from bottom to top close to zipper teeth.

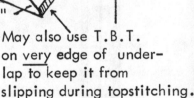

5/8"

May also use T.B.T. on very edge of under-lap to keep it from slipping during topstitching.

NOTE: Do not stitch through T.B.T. Remove and discard tape before pressing or laundering.

5. Stitch overlap in place. Use 3/4" Scotch Magic Tape to hold overlap in place with 3/8" extending over edge. Use other edge as a guide to straight topstitching. Stitch from bottom to top.

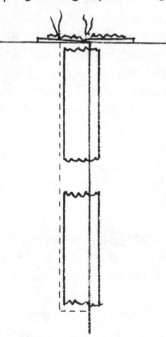

NOTE: When approaching top of zipper, avoid crooked stitches by lowering needle into fabric, lifting presser foot, and by unzipping zipper to get slider out of way. Continue stitching to top.

# TWO NIFTY PATCH POCKET TRICKS

## FIRST TRICK

1. Stitch pocket and lining together all the way around and trim with pinking shears. Slash corners.

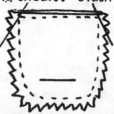

2. Snip a 1-1/2" hole in the lining at the pocket bottom. Turn right side out through hole and press. Tuck a small piece of fusible web under the hole and fuse closed.


## SECOND TRICK

1. Place 1/4" wide strip of fusible web under pocket edge.

2. Steam baste* in place to prevent slippage while topstitching. This also keeps matched plaids from moving.

* Steam basting means to slightly fuse. It is not permanent. Use 1 - 3 seconds of steam, heat and pressure. If for some reason pockets must be moved, pull apart and brush away web residue.

# TAKE YOUR SEWING ONE STEP FURTHER

The more you experience in sewing, the faster you will learn and understand the many concepts that become your sewing foundation. For example, all that we write is not necessarily original, but we hope it is written in a way you may find easier to understand. After all, the more sources you read for reference, the more things seem to click. We have a theory about learning to sew -- it's like learning to play the piano. You simply can't take one lesson or read one piano instruction book and find you can play, let alone compose your own music. The FASTEST way to learn to sew super well is to concentrate on sewing for one full year. Read as much as you can, and take as many classes as possible.

Why not start a sewing book collection to match your cookbook collection? Or... if the budget doesn't permit... spend time at the public library.

We all need a boost once in awhile. Both of us subscribe to our "incentive to sew" magazines --- Vogue Patterns and McCalls Patterns. They are well photographed, include drawings of each design and tell you what fabrics they used to get that gorgeous look (and why not copy occasionally -- use their expertise to help you get started). They also give sewing tips relating to "current" fashion.

Also, treat yourself to some "gourmet" sewing classes. Of course, if we are in your city, please come to our seminars! If not, find two or three local teachers and learn from each.

We feel very strongly about wanting you to really LIKE sewing. Therefore, we want to recommend some other references that we have enjoyed reading:
1. Coats & Clark's Sewing Book
2. Simplicity Sewing Book
3. Vogue Sewing Book

All of these books are easy to find. Others that you will truly enjoy, but that are harder to find, are the following, written by people very knowledgeable

about their specialties.  They have researched a single
area of sewing  and have taught so many classes that they
anticipate your questions in their books.

Husband pleasers will enjoy one of the best books
we know on menswear, <u>Men's Tailoring for the Home Sewer</u>.
Author Beverly Smith has trained with tailors.  Write
her at 1057 Landova Drive, Escondido, CA  92027.

How about using fabric in your home?  Judy Lindahl,
past educational representative for Simplicity Pattern
Co., has put together a wealth of information on home
decorating in her two books, <u>Decorating with Fabric</u>
(revised $4.95) and <u>The Shade Book</u> (revised $4.95).  To
order, write P.O. Box 8422, Portland, OR  97207.  Include
75¢ per order for postage and handling.

If you are interested in design and decide to go
that one step further, try Virginia Nastiuk's books
<u>Personal Pattern Development</u>.  Books I, II and III are
$7.95 each.  The first introduces pattern making and
covers fitting, and the last two cover design.  For
information, write 17126 North Road, Bothell, WA 98011.

We are great experimentalists.  If you have any
questions or new PAINLESS IDEAS, please write to us.

# TGIF - Thank Goodness It's Finished!

Additional copies of <u>Mother Pletsch's Painless Sewing and Pretty Pati's Perfect Pattern Primer</u> may be found in your local fabric or department store. If not, write P.O. Box 8422, Portland, Ore. 97207. Price is $4.50. Please include 75¢ for postage and handling.